M000074922

THE TEENAGE PRAYER EXPERIMENT NOTEBOOK

Miranda & Noah Threlfall-Holmes

SPCK

First published in Great Britain in 2015

Society for Promoting Christian Knowledge
36 Causton Street
London SW1P 4ST
www.spckpublishing.co.uk

British Library Cataloguing-in-Publication Data
A catalogue record for this book is available from the British Library

ISBN 978–0–281–07257–6
eBook ISBN 978–0–281–07258–3

Designed and typeset by Penguin Boy Ltd (www.penguinboy.net)
First printed in Great Britain by Ashford Colour Press
Subsequently digitally printed in Great Britain

eBook by Graphicraft Limited, Hong Kong

Produced on paper from sustainable forests

Contents

CONTENTS

Introduction

This is not a book to teach teenagers about prayer. It is a book to encourage teenagers to try prayer out for themselves.

There were several different reasons for writing this book. It began when two brothers, members of our local church, were confirmed, and I went to the local Christian bookshop to buy confirmation presents for them. As regular churchgoers, the family already had several Bibles, introductions to Christianity, etc., so what I wanted to give the boys was a simple guide to beginning to establish a prayer life. To my astonishment, I could find nothing in that category at all, and the bookshop staff were unable to suggest anything that they could order in. I went home, and over tea that afternoon told the family how disappointing my trip had been. 'Maybe you should write one, then,' my husband suggested. And over the course of that meal, the idea grew. By using a blog we could very easily write something online, and Noah agreed that if I came up with some ideas, he would try them out and review them. So, later that evening, the 'Teenage Prayer Experiment' blog was born.

From the beginning, we were clear about what we did *not* want to write. It seems to us that too many Christian books and resources aimed at children, tweenagers and teenagers are didactic. They assume that the author – the adult – is the expert, and that the expert's job is to impart knowledge to his or her younger audience. This stands in stark contrast to modern educational psychology and methods, which emphasize how important experiential learning is. And my own observation is that this is particularly the case with teenagers: they will rebel at anything that smacks of being told what to think, and are at a life stage where experimentation is both natural and the most effective way for them to learn. My own faith, too, is primarily about encountering the living God and being transformed by that encounter, rather than being centred on learning facts about God.

So we had two guiding principles for this project. The first was that it was to be fully co-authored between us. We were determined not to make this a book by an adult expert for a teenage subject. We wanted rather to model a genuinely equal collaboration between disciples of two different ages. There was no sense in which I was the 'prayer expert'; I was simply suggesting, from my knowledge of and training in the Christian tradition, some ideas that it might be worth trying. It was only as Noah tested the ideas that we could tell if they were any good, or how they might need to be modified.

Second, we were sure that the word 'experiment' was key. We have deliberately used the scientific vocabulary of experimentation, because it implies that these experiments will be undertaken with an open mind and that the results will be judged on their own merits.

My own spiritual journey, particularly my conversion at university, has led me to believe that becoming a Christian is not primarily something you can learn about academically, it is something you have to experience from the inside. The way to encounter God and to find out about praying is by giving it a try – 'taste, and see that the Lord is good', as the Bible puts it. So from my point of view, I wanted to create a resource that would not teach young people *about* prayer, but instead would encourage them to *try praying*. From Noah's point of view, he came to this project unsure of his own faith, having been taken to church since birth (he was born while I was studying for ordination at theological college). He was willing to experiment, but unwilling to have anything imposed upon him. So for both of us, the idea of an open-ended series of experiments, with no pre-determined outcome beyond writing up whatever happened, was the heart of the plan.

Since beginning the blog, we have been astonished and delighted at how widely it has been used, and at the overwhelmingly positive reception it has been given. Within weeks, we learned that it was providing a curriculum for youth groups around the country. Parents told me how their children, resistant to any parental religious pressure, were nevertheless prepared to try out a prayer experiment from the blog. And RE teachers have told us that we have provided a rare resource for the new curriculum emphasis on religious experience. Most importantly, as teenagers (and some younger children) tried the experiments and began to send us their feedback, I was repeatedly overwhelmed by the honesty, clarity and thoughtfulness with which they discussed their religious experiences and whether a particular prayer method was for them. I wish we could find a way of encouraging adults in our churches to discuss and think about their prayer lives so honestly and openly.

So we very much hope that this book will be a great gift for confirmation candidates, which is where it all began. And we hope too that it will be of use to any teenager who wants to give prayer a go and maybe compare notes with other teens; that it will be enjoyed by youth groups working through it together; and that it will provide a 'virtual peer group' for teens who may find they are the only Christian they know, or the only teenager in their church.

However you use it, and whoever you are, I hope you enjoy it. More than that, I hope that it helps you to meet the living God in prayer.

Miranda Threlfall-Holmes
Durham

How to use this book

This is not a book to tell you how to pray. It is a book of experiments in prayer for you to try for yourself.

It includes space for you to make notes on how you found each experiment, and notes from other experimenters so that you can compare your experiences and reactions with those of other teenagers who have tried them out.

There will be experiments that you like, and no doubt ones that you don't like too. You can only know which are which by trying them out. You'll see from the other experimenters' notes that different people like different things, and some have also made suggestions for improvements or variations to the experiments.

You don't have to read this book from front to back, or try the experiments in any particular order, or even try all of the experiments. We have put them in this order so that different styles of prayer are mixed up: if you start at page 1 and go through to the end, you will find that an active or creative prayer idea is followed by a more reflective one, and so on. But you can choose to do them in any order, or just pick out the ones that sound most interesting.

For each experiment, there are four parts.

First there is a brief introduction to the prayer idea being suggested, and why and how it has been used in the Christian spiritual tradition. Next comes the experiment itself: what to do, any equipment you will need, where to do it. After that you will find space for your own notes on what using that prayer idea was like: what happened, how did it make you feel, would you do anything differently if you were repeating the experiment? And finally there are notes from other experimenters, so you can compare your experience with theirs.

It is up to you whether you read the other experimenters' notes before doing the experiment yourself, or not. You may find that reading their notes helps you identify the experiments that sound like they would most appeal to you. Or you may prefer to try the experiments without being influenced by what anyone else thought, and then compare notes later.

The most important thing is that you actually try the experiments out! We have both found that the only way to tell what praying in a particular way is like is to try it. It is no good just reading about it. So even if you want to read this book through before starting, do then choose one experiment, put the book down, and give it a try.

We hope you enjoy experimenting!

Noah and Miranda

Prayer den

A place for praying

Many people find it easier to pray in church, or in a chapel, than at home. There seems to be something helpful about deliberately going to a place that is set aside for prayer. In the past, wealthy Christians with grand houses would often have a chapel in their home, or a small room that was set aside for reading the Bible and praying. As well as the convenience of having somewhere at home, there is also a difference between praying in a big, public building and in a small, private space.

Praying in a big space has the advantage of making you feel part of something bigger than yourself. Huge, soaring ceilings are designed to lift your eyes and mind to God's majesty, and make you feel very small in comparison. And praying in a public building makes the important point that we are not just individual Christians, but part of the worldwide Church of Christ.

On the other hand, a small space of your own can feel much safer and more intimate. It can be somewhere to feel private with God, somewhere you feel safe to be yourself without having to think about what other people might be thinking of you, and somewhere it feels like God comes to meet you, rather than you having to go to meet God.

Few of us have space for a chapel in our homes, but you could make a prayer corner in your room. As you go through this book trying the various experiments, why not keep some of the things you make and put them together on a shelf or windowsill in your room? Then you will build up your own personal collection of prayer objects and reminders, and create a prayer corner of your own.

The experiment

THIS EXPERIMENT TAKES THE IDEA OF MAKING A PRAYER CORNER A STEP FURTHER. THE IDEA IS TO MAKE A DEN, A SMALL ENCLOSED SPACE TO PRAY IN – JUST BIG ENOUGH FOR ONE OR MAYBE TWO PEOPLE.

First, you'll need to decide where to build the den. Could you make it in the corner of your bedroom? Or maybe in a family room, the shed or the garage? If it is summer, you might want to build one outside. This could either be something that just stays up for an afternoon, or a semi-permanent structure, whatever suits the space you have available.

The easiest way to build it is to pitch a tent! You may have a tent for the garden, or do you have a younger brother or sister who has a pop-up play tent that you could borrow?

Here are some other ideas: a bottom bunk bed, with sheets or blankets clipped to the bunk above; a clothes airer; some rearranged pieces of furniture (chests of drawers, chairs, etc.); a large cardboard box from something like a fridge or washing machine; or underneath a table.

Then cover your chosen framework with sheets, blankets, duvets, etc., to make a completely enclosed space. You want it to be comfortable to sit in for a reasonable length of time, so cover the floor with pillows, cushions, beanbags, etc.

PRAYER DEN

Now you get to decide how to decorate the inside of your den! People who have tried this particularly liked having fairy lights or a lava lamp in the den. Or you could take a torch in with you. Just be careful only to use a low-wattage lamp that doesn't get hot, to avoid any risk of fire.

You may also want to add other things – maybe items from your prayer corner, bunting, or a rug. Make a space that feels snug and secure, somewhere you will enjoy sitting in and that feels very personal to you.

Once you have built the den, it is time to start using it to pray in. Just go in, sit down, and imagine that God is in there with you. You can either just sit quietly imagining yourself in God's presence, or talk with God, or say prayers that you know such as the Lord's Prayer. Or why not try combining this experiment with others, and doing one or two of the other prayer activities suggested here in the den?

Feedback

WHEN I TRIED THIS EXPERIMENT, I FOUND . . .

AS I MADE THE PRAYER DEN, I FELT . . .

PRAYING IN THIS SPACE MADE ME FEEL . . .

THE THING I LIKED BEST ABOUT IT WAS . . .

THINGS I WOULD TRY CHANGING NEXT TIME:

MARKS OUT OF 10:

Noah's review: 9/10

I used a pop-up tent in my garden, filled with duvets, cushions and with some fairy lights hanging from the roof with string. My cat came in too. Having the cat in there was lovely, it was something warm to snuggle up to and it reminded me of how good God is and what he creates. I lay down with a duvet over me which felt warm and comfortable.

I started off by praying about my family and situations abroad – normal kind of stuff. Then, because I was outside in the garden, I heard some teenagers shouting in the street, and that started me praying for my local area too. So I found that being somewhere different – in the tent outside – made me pray for different things.

I really liked the fact it was small. In church, although it's a nice atmosphere, it can feel too spacious: there's a sense of pressure that I can't really describe from being somewhere so big and public. But being in my room can feel stressful because I often see things on the floor, or pieces of work I haven't done yet, that distract me. So it felt really nice being in the tent. The best thing was the gentleness of it, I felt safe with just the background noises going on outside and the warm cat snuggling up and the gentle chirping of the birds and the leaves on the trees.

Sometimes when I pray I imagine God with angels, etc. receiving all the prayers like emails or something on some amazing out-of-this-world piece of technology. Somehow being in the tent I found I imagined them in the tree outside rather than up in the clouds, so it was like they were closer.

When I do this again I'll use more fairy lights — they're quite subtle lights, and it's easier to pray when the atmosphere is right. Doing it outside with the tent was good, but next time I'll try inside and I'll just use cushions from the sofa and duvets and blankets to make a den. Next time I want to sleep in it.

Other experimenters' notes

10/10 – We loved praying in the den together. It was quite a small space, so we were quite bunched up! It was very calming and atmospheric, and felt very warm, safe and enclosed. Also, being in there together made us think more about God as a friend. (Anna, 16, and Rachel, 15)

10/10 – IT MADE ME THINK: NORMALLY, YOU PRAY WITH SOLID WALLS AROUND YOU, WHICH MIGHT SET BOUNDARIES ON WHAT YOU CAN DO, BUT IN THE DEN I FELT I COULD DO WHATEVER I WANTED. IT FELT A BIT LIKE GOD WAS IN THERE WITH ME – IT DIDN'T FEEL LIKE I WAS ALONE, EVEN THOUGH I WAS. (JONNY, 14)

10/10 – There's only one thing I would change. I like to write stuff down, so next time I would make sure I took a notebook or something in as well. (Emily, 17)

Bedroom door prayers

Making an entrance

What does it say on your bedroom door? 'Keep Out'? Maybe your name? Or is your door covered in posters representing who you are and what your interests are?

What about your front door? It might have just a number, maybe a 'Welcome' doormat. Or maybe that door too is decorated, at least sometimes in the year? Balloons tied on the door, or to the gatepost, for a party tell people to expect fun inside: a Christmas wreath on the door makes the house feel festive and welcoming. What we put at entrances sets an atmosphere.

In many religious traditions, written prayers or short blessings are put on doorways. As well as asking God to bless the house or room, the idea is that every time you enter or leave the house, you are reminded to pray. You don't even have to consciously say the prayer each time, you just see it and notice it as you are passing.

The experiment

TRY WRITING DOORWAY PRAYERS FOR YOUR BEDROOM DOOR. LET'S DO TWO: ONE FOR OUTSIDE YOUR DOOR, THAT YOU'LL SEE WHEN YOU GO IN, AND ONE FOR THE INSIDE, THAT YOU'LL SEE EVERY TIME YOU LEAVE. (IF YOU TEND TO LEAVE YOUR BEDROOM DOOR OPEN, PUT THIS ONE NEXT TO THE DOOR FRAME OR LIGHT SWITCH ON THE INSIDE OF THE ROOM INSTEAD.)

1. Think about what you would like a prayer or blessing that you see going in to your room to say. You might be going in to go to bed, or to be on your own. You might just be popping in to get a jumper, sitting down to do homework, feeling sad or lonely or wanting to curl up with a good book or a computer game.

    Perhaps: 'God bless this room'.

    Or: 'God, be with me'.

    Or: 'God bless all my thoughts and dreams'.

    Or: 'God's peace be in this place'.

    You could choose one of those, or write your own.

2. And what would you want to pray for as you leave your room? You might be leaving for school; going out briefly to get a drink; about to visit family, who you may or may not want to see at that moment.

    Perhaps: 'God, be with me wherever I go'.

    Or: 'God bless me'.

    Or: 'God grant me patience and peace'.

    Or: 'God, protect and surround me with your love'.

11

3. When you've decided what to put on each sign, write or print them out. Mount the signs on a piece of paper or card, and decorate them as much as you like. Make them something you will enjoy seeing. And make sure the writing is quite big, so you can read them as you approach the door. Then stick them to your door, or the door frame, where you will see them every time you go in or out.

4. Leave them there for at least a week. For the first day or two, deliberately say the prayers – either out loud, or just quietly to yourself – every time you see them. After that, you will probably find you hear them in your head anyway, but just make sure you notice them each time you go in or out.

If you like this idea, you could always do it for other doors too. The front door, the bathroom door, the kitchen door? Maybe other family members would like prayers for their doors too?

Feedback

WHEN I TRIED THIS EXPERIMENT, I FOUND ...

SEEING THE PRAYERS MADE ME FEEL ...

AFTER THEY'D BEEN UP FOR A FEW DAYS ...

THE THING I LIKED BEST ABOUT IT WAS ...

THINGS I WOULD TRY CHANGING NEXT TIME:

MARKS OUT OF 10:

Feedback

WHEN I TRIED THIS EXPERIMENT, I FOUND ...

SEEING THE PRAYERS MADE ME FEEL ...

AFTER THEY'D BEEN UP FOR A FEW DAYS ...

THE THING I LIKED BEST ABOUT IT WAS ...

THINGS I WOULD TRY CHANGING NEXT TIME:

MARKS OUT OF 10:

Noah's review: 4/10

I made two Post-It notes for my door. As I came in I had 'God be in this place', and going out I had 'God be with me wherever I go'. I read them each time I passed, though the sticky notes fell off the door after two days! But by that time it came naturally to keep saying it each time I went through the door. The effect wasn't very noticeable though. I prefer the activities where you interact with something else. Just saying something was not as powerful. It did make me think about God though, not every time I walked in but quite often. When I went to bed, for example, I found I usually said a prayer because it had reminded me to. I think this may have worked better if I had spent more time making the signs.

Other experimenters' notes

8/10 – I have found this really helpful and inspiring. I used two index cards that I had spare from making my revision notes, and I wrote the prayers on those and stuck them up on either side of my door. I didn't decorate them, as when I'd written the words I wanted they looked just how I wanted them to.

For the one that I'd see going out of the room, I wrote a prayer about body image and making sure that I remember to live every day as if it were going to be my last, and to remember that I am fearfully and wonderfully made.

For the one going in, I was inspired by my exams, and the prayer I wrote reminds me when I enter my room to appreciate all my opportunities, and work not for anyone else but for myself; and to make sure I study, as tomorrow is made of today.

I really like having the prayers up on my door. Whenever I go through the door, I notice them, and at first I think 'what's that on my door?' when they catch my eye. Then I remember, and read them again, and I find they really inspire me. They remind me of the things I wrote on them to be reminded of, and I've also found they've made me kind of feel a bit more connected with God. It reminds me that God's with me. It really worked! (Jasmine, 14)

2/10 – I DIDN'T REALLY WANT A PRAYER UP ABOVE MY ROOM FOR EVERYONE TO SEE: I'D RATHER KEEP PRAYER AS A PRIVATE THING JUST FOR ME. I CAN SEE HOW THIS MIGHT WORK FOR OTHER PEOPLE, REMINDING YOU TO PRAY, BUT IT WASN'T FOR ME. (EMILY, 17)

6/10 – The one for going in was quite good. I made it on gold card, just saying 'God give me peace in this room', and it just went right in my head. Every time I saw it I thought, 'Oh, yeah', and remembered it again. The one going out asked God to help me do well at school, but that one wasn't in such a good place so I don't see it so much.

The signs have come down and gone back up a few times. The tape holding them up fails every so often, and then sometimes I've rearranged things, but I've always stuck them back up.

The only thing is, it was a bit weird having what I was praying for displayed for people walking past the room to see. But it soon just became part of the scenery so I've stopped noticing it so much, and stopped being self-conscious about it. (Luke, 16)

6/10

- I like the idea and can't wait to put it up on my wall.
- It was really fun, and it was really cool and creative.
- It's like we can put a bit of church in our bedrooms!
- I think it was quite peaceful.

(Members of 'Encounter', All Saints Church, High Wycombe)

7/10 – I HAD A PIECE OF PAPER ON THE CURTAIN COVERING MY DOOR. AFTER A WHILE, IT KEPT GETTING IN THE WAY SO I REMOVED IT BUT I HAD GOT USED TO SAYING IT IN MY HEAD AND I SAY THE PRAYER GOING OUT OF THE DOOR AUTOMATICALLY NOW. (HANNAH, 10)

9/10 – I found a sizeable piece of card and painted the background purple. Then I chose the line 'God grant me patience and peace', and I painted it in all sorts of different colours and fonts, each in a different way. Then I painted my hand blue and made a handprint in one corner, and then put gold glitter all over the whole thing.

It was nice and peaceful doing it, because it was something I've done, and it was nice to choose the colours and experiment with all the different styles of writing. The key words stand out so it makes you notice them. (Catherine, 15)

Minecraft church

A place to pray

Although we can pray to God anywhere, you might find going somewhere special helps you to focus your mind. This might just be somewhere in your home where you always go to pray, a particular chair or corner of your room.

Many people associate praying with going to church or another special place such as a chapel, cathedral, shrine or quiet garden. Somewhere they can feel at peace, or closer to God, or just somewhere that is different from everyday life. It can be especially helpful if it is a place that is specially set aside for prayer, and where people have prayed for years.

All through Christian history, people have built small chapels in their houses, roadside shrines, local churches and huge cathedrals, all with the aim of making a place that helps you to focus on praying by taking you outside of normal life for a while.

Virtual worlds

Noah spends large amounts of time on the computer game Minecraft. So we wondered – could Minecraft, or another virtual world like Second Life, be somewhere you can pray? Could you make a special place to pray in a virtual world, and what would it be like to pray there?

Like a shrine or church, virtual world computer games have the advantage that they are somewhere outside your day-to-day life. They are places where people go to get away from their usual lives for a bit, places where you might meet friends, imagine yourself differently, and try new things.

A game like Minecraft also has the advantage of being a very creative place, somewhere you are free to express yourself in building and where you can build almost anything you can imagine. So it is a good place to experiment and try things out, and you might find that being in Minecraft makes you feel much more imaginative.

When people tried this, they often found that they felt a much greater sense of ownership of the prayer space, because they had made it themselves. Praying in a space you have made yourself might make you pray in a different way. For example, we found that several people ended up leading worship for others, literally taking charge of the use of that worship space. Praying in a virtual world led some people to try out different roles in leading worship, from the vicar to the organist!

The experiment

THIS EXPERIMENT INVOLVES CREATING A PRAYER
SPACE IN A VIRTUAL WORLD BUILDING GAME THAT
YOU ENJOY AND ARE FAMILIAR WITH, SUCH AS MINECRAFT.

First, think about what your ideal place for prayer would be.

Where would it be?

What views would it have?

What would it look like?

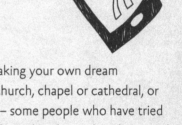

How big would it be?

What would it have inside it?

What would you do there?

Now go online and have a go at making your own dream
prayer space. It might be a virtual church, chapel or cathedral, or
it could look completely different – some people who have tried
this have made very traditional-looking churches, others have made
anything from floating platforms in glass boxes to tiny houses.

One thing to watch out for is the combat that is part of some
versions of these games. It doesn't create a very prayerful atmosphere
if you are having to keep fighting off zombies or giant spiders. So
we would suggest that you do this in Creative rather than Survival
mode, or on Peaceful settings, to avoid monsters disturbing you.

Once you've built your prayer space, try going into it, in your virtual
character, and spend some time praying there. Is it any different from
being in a chapel, church, or prayer space in the real world? If so, how?

Feedback

WHEN I TRIED MAKING A PRAYER PLACE, I FOUND ...

PRAYING IN THE PLACE I'D MADE, I ...

THE THING I LIKED BEST ABOUT IT WAS ...

THINGS I WOULD TRY CHANGING NEXT TIME:

MARKS OUT OF 10:

Noah's review: 7/10

I didn't want to build a massive cathedral but I wanted something fairly big. I made it look like a traditional church. I was sort of trying to create my version of our local church: it's nice, and makes me think about God, because it's got the right kind of atmosphere.

So I made a church building, with a nave and the altar, choir stalls, at least 50 pews, a bell tower and stained glass windows. I built it facing east–west, so the sun would come up through the big window over the altar.

I was thinking about the stuff in the church when I was putting in the details — the pews, and the pulpit, and so on. I was thinking about how it is all designed to face the front and wondering whether that is a good thing or not. It makes you focus on what the vicar has to say, but because it makes everyone focus on the front they might miss some of the other lovely bits of the church that people put lots of effort into building.

When I'd built the altar, I suddenly thought of getting a vicar skin (costume) for my character, so I did. It just felt natural to be the vicar since I was building the church.

Then I led a short service in the church as the vicar. It was just me and my younger brother, with him being the congregation. First, we sang a verse of a hymn. Then I went up into the pulpit and told the story of Jesus asking the Samaritan woman for water at the well (we'd done that reading in Junior Church that morning), and I ended by asking my brother a question about the reading. He answered, and then he left and I went and stood in front of the altar looking at the big window. Then I took my hands off the keyboard and said a few prayers.

Having built the church I wanted to use it, and role-playing being the vicar seemed the best way of doing that. It felt very natural leading a service for my brother who was there in the game too. There was something about having built the church myself that made me feel like it was my place where I was responsible for leading the prayers, not just doing them.

Other experimenters' notes

8/10 – I made this to feel more like a home than a building you had to go to: somewhere that felt warm and quite back to basics. So it was just a rectangular house, and inside it had two flowerpots and was lit by four torches. It was built into the side of a mountain just over a river, partially overhanging the water.

Making it felt good – it meant I knew I had something I'd created myself. And it felt comfortable praying in it because it was my place.

As I pictured myself being there and praying there, I found that took away all my problems and worries in this world and meant I felt like I only had the worries that I had in the Minecraft world, which isn't many. (Reuben, 13)

4/10 – I BUILT A CHURCH THAT WAS ON A WORLD WHERE BOTH ME AND MY FRIEND COULD USE IT. THE IDEA WAS THAT WE COULD USE IT TOGETHER. HOWEVER, WHEN I TRIED TO PRAY IN IT ON MY OWN I FOUND IT A BIT STRANGE.

I PUT VILLAGERS IN TO BE THE CONGREGATION AND A PRIEST (A VILLAGER) AT THE FRONT BEHIND THE ALTAR, BUT HE RAN AWAY WHEN I OPENED THE GATE TO LET MY DOG IN, SO I USED MY DOG INSTEAD.

THE DOG WAS MUCH BETTER BECAUSE IT WAS A THING TO KEEP MY ATTENTION ON – THERE WERE ALSO A LOT OF PIGS OUTSIDE SNORTING LOUDLY.

IF I TRY IT AGAIN I MIGHT TRY TO MAKE THE CHURCH BIGGER AND MORE MAJESTIC TO MAKE IT OF HIGHER SPIRITUAL VALUE FOR ME. I ALSO TRIED TO DO THIS IN THE SIMILAR GAME BLOCKHEADS, BUT THAT DIDN'T REALLY WORK FOR ME EITHER. (DANIEL, 11)

8/10 – I'd give this 8 because it was quite fun and creative making it, and then you can calm down from anything that's worrying you when you go into it. Because your mind is in a creative mood when you are in Minecraft it is easier to think and pray.

I did this with my brother Ben. We made a big church, a big rectangle with a roof and two floors. It had a font, organ, altar, pews, a pulpit, hymn boards and a cross. We called it the Church of St Steve of Minecraft, and on the top floor we built a shrine. We had quite a big discussion about how to make the altar, and ended up using two Ender portals because they had the right sort of lacy effect, as if they had a cloth over them.

When it came to praying in it, we got all the villagers into the pews and choir stalls, and I went into the pulpit and prayed. I prayed for the things that the people in Minecraft would need; for them, and their enemies like the Creepers, and their crops and so on. Doing it in Minecraft meant I thought of the things that were relevant there, but then I prayed for those sorts of things in real life too – people with enemies, and not enough food to eat, and animals.

My brother was the organist, so his character sat at the organ and he wiggled his fingers in real life to be 'playing' the organ while we all sang lots of hymns.

I might make a Sunday School area next, for the small villagers. And I've had an idea for a church BBQ, because you can get the right kind of meat for that in the game. (Phoebe, 11, with her brother Ben, 8)

9/10 - I really liked this idea, because you can have fun building it and then it felt good because it's a place that I built, so it can be exactly as I want it. I made a little chapel in the ground with colourful blocks, with just a kneeler in the middle and a table at one end. For some of the time I stood on the kneeler, and for some I crouched on it. Praying there felt basically the same as praying in real life, but it was more entertaining. (Edward, 14)

Praying with your whole body

The mind/body connection

How much do you think about what you do with your body when you pray? Scientists are continually finding more connections between our bodies and our minds. We are not just a mind in a body, like a computer in a case. Our bodies are part of us, and what we do with our bodies can shape our thinking.

Try this: smile. You actually feel happier when you make the muscle movements that are a smile, even if you are just acting.

We don't tend to think much about what we are doing with our bodies when we are praying, though you might well remember being told at primary school to pray 'Hands together, eyes closed'. The idea of that is to stop distractions. Hands together means you aren't fiddling, eyes closed means you aren't distracted by what you can see around you.

In some churches, you will find that people stand, sit and kneel at different parts of the service. It can be confusing if you go to a church you aren't used to, as not all churches choose the same posture for the same bits!

Prayer positions

How many different physical ways of praying can you think of?

Originally, in Roman times, people seem to have stood to pray, with their arms outstretched. If you go to many churches, the posture of the priest during the communion prayer is a descendant of this.

Kneeling became fashionable in the Middle Ages. It was a position that people were used to because you knelt before a lord, or the king. Kneeling was used because as people began to have a more personal idea of God, they related to God as they would to their social superior. A similar theme can be seen in other cultures. Muslims, for example, bow, kneel and then bow their heads to the ground in prayer, which again imitates the kind of posture used in the presence of a king or superior in Eastern medieval culture.

In some times and places, people lie face down on the floor to pray. This is called prostration, and it is usually kept for particularly serious times of prayer. In some churches now, it is used on Good Friday, or at the ordination of new clergy. In the past, monks or nuns might pray all night lying on the floor before taking vows to join the monastery, and a knight might do the same before a battle.

Nowadays, the most common posture for prayer is sitting down. Differences are mostly about what you do with your hands. Clasped together? Flat together? Open on your knees, as if you are waiting to receive something from God? In the air, as if you are carried away at a rock concert or celebrating a goal?

The experiment

IN THIS EXPERIMENT, YOU CAN TRY OUT SEVERAL DIFFERENT POSTURES FOR PRAYER, AND SEE HOW THEY MAKE YOU FEEL ABOUT THE RELATIONSHIP BETWEEN YOU AND GOD.

1. Go to your room, or somewhere you know you won't be disturbed, so you don't feel embarrassed at being found in a variety of strange positions! Then try standing, with your arms out (like a priest at the altar). Imagine you are standing before God. How does it feel to be in front of God like this?

2. Next, kneel down, either on one or both knees. This is rather like kneeling before the monarch to be knighted; or pleading with a lord for some favour, or mercy. Imagine you are kneeling in front of God: how does it feel?

3. Now lie down, flat on your front. Legs together, arms outstretched – a bit like a lying-down crucifix. Are you lying in front of God? How does that feel? Or are you imagining what it was like to be Christ on the cross?

4. Now sit on a chair, or on the side of your bed. Imagine Jesus sitting next to you. How does it feel to be talking to God in this position? If you like, try out some different hand positions too.

5. If your body comes up with other positions to try, then try those out too. Think about how each position makes you feel, and how it makes you feel in relation to God if you imagine God there in the room with you.

Feedback

WHEN I TRIED THIS EXPERIMENT, I FOUND ...

STANDING MADE ME FEEL ...

KNEELING MADE ME FEEL ...

LYING DOWN MADE ME FEEL ...

SITTING MADE ME FEEL ...

THE THING I LIKED BEST ABOUT IT WAS ...

THINGS I WOULD TRY CHANGING NEXT TIME:

MARKS OUT OF 10:

Noah's review: 9.5/10

I used the different positions and thought about God being in front of me: and it was the WEIRDEST experience. Even though I had my eyes closed I imagined this big light; and there was – hard to explain it – God standing there. And so I didn't say anything because if God was really there I think I'd be too scared to.

I tried standing first. It ached a bit as I don't like standing still for long, but it was probably the one where if God was actually in front of me, I'd be most shocked. If I was sitting down I'd feel more relaxed, small and safe, but standing felt more vulnerable – vulnerable to God's power. If you were standing before God what would he say to you? Look at all these wrong things you've done? God always expects better, it says so in the Bible. When I was standing I felt like God was telling me off.

Kneeling didn't really feel right: I wouldn't kneel in front of God, I'd rather stand or preferably sit down. When I was kneeling it felt like an interview with God, it was traumatizing: I felt small, with no protection. I imagined a picture in my head, in heaven – kneel here in front of God's big desk – and he starts interviewing you and telling you all the wrong things you've done in your life and the few good things you've done. And all the time I'm hoping God will let me into heaven – which he probably would, because he forgives, but it was still pretty horrible.

Sitting down was the easiest, because it was much more relaxing. I didn't have such a strong picture in my head as I felt much more relaxed. God was there – I imagined the bright light – but I was just getting on with praying in front of God. So I prayed about things that were happening in the world.

Lying down was really strange but definitely my favourite because of what happened. For the first minute or so I was just settling down and trying to close down my senses and stuff and imagine God, and so I was saying the Lord's Prayer. And then – a bit like that bit in the Bible where God calls Jonah – it was as if there was a bright light over my bed, and a voice saying the Lord's Prayer with me. That only lasted quite briefly and I lay there for a bit longer hoping it would come back but nothing more happened. That was a lovely experience and I'd really like it to happen again.

Other experimenters' notes

8/10 – First I tried standing up, with my hands behind my back. I was doing this with a friend, and we talked in turns and prayed together almost like a conversation. I found it quite thought-provoking: it wasn't at all how I'd usually pray. But I did find I fidgeted quite a lot and couldn't stand still for very long.

After that, I tried kneeling down. My dad and I used to kneel for prayers before bed when I was little, so because that was something from my childhood, it reminded me of the sort of things I used to pray for and was thankful for then.

It was a nice day, so for the lying down I went outside. I lay on my back on the grass, kept my eyes open, and looked around at everything. It was lovely to be in God's world, and see everything and how beautiful it was. It reminded me of all the things to be thankful for – the birds singing, the trees. The only problem was I was a bit fidgety as I'm not keen on bugs and dirt, so I kept worrying what was getting in my hair! With hindsight I should have used a blanket to lie on. But even so, it was very relaxing.

I really enjoyed trying this. It gave me a new perspective, new ideas for ways of praying and a new insight into myself and how I pray. I liked lying down outside best. Kneeling was more normal, so it didn't really have that sense of trying something different. (Rachel, 15)

8/10 – I FOUND THAT FOR ME, A SITTING POSITION ON THE FLOOR WITH LEGS CROSSED WAS THE BEST. WHEN I WAS SITTING I FOUND I SAW A BRIGHT LIGHT IN MY HEAD AS IF GOD WAS IN FRONT OF ME, BUT THE SENSATION WAS A BIT OVERWHELMING SO I OPENED MY EYES AND STOPPED CONCENTRATING, AND THE FEELING STOPPED.

I LIKED ALL THE POSTURES EXCEPT KNEELING AND LYING ON MY FRONT, BUT I LIKED SITTING THE BEST. I MIGHT LIE FLAT ON MY BACK NEXT TIME.

IT MADE ME FEEL KIND OF WEIRD BUT ALSO SPIRITUAL. I FELT A CONNECTION WITH THE SPIRIT. (DANIEL, 11)

8/10 – Lying down was much more comfortable than standing or kneeling. They felt much more formal, and I found that I felt a slight vulnerability praying in that sort of formal situation. Whereas when I was comfortable I found it easier to pray, and I felt more of a bond of friendship with God, rather than God as a more distant Father. It was good trying different positions, as it helped me realize there isn't just one way to pray. (Anna, 16)

ACTS

ADORATION, CONFESSION, THANKSGIVING, SUPPLICATION

The four food groups of prayer

You are probably familiar with the idea that eating a healthy diet means eating a balance of foods from the different food groups. One way of thinking about staying spiritually healthy is to make sure that your prayer 'diet' is also balanced. A popular way of thinking of the different food groups of prayer is ACTS. This stands for:

1. Adoration (adoring God, standing in awe at God, praising God)

2. Confession (admitting all the ways we are not perfect, and resolving to do better)

3. Thanksgiving (saying thank you to God for all that we have and are)

4. Supplication (asking God for things we need, asking for help for ourselves or others).

The idea is that a balanced prayer life consists of all four elements. Many people find that they actually do mainly number 4, with not very much of 1, 2 or 3. But a balanced diet of prayer will have all the different elements.

The next four experiments focus on one of these elements at a time. Often, you will want to make sure you do all four each time you pray. But for now, we will split them out and look at each one individually.

1 ADORATION

Adoration is thinking about, contemplating, how wonderful God is. It's rather like looking out at a beautiful view, or enjoying eating something delicious: you're not so much talking about how great the thing is, you are just enjoying it and being aware of how wonderful it is.

What reminds you how amazing God is? For some people, it might be being at the top of a high mountain, or seeing a beautiful sunset, or the ocean waves, or a huge storm. You might find yourself filled with a sense of awe at wild animals, or tiny insects, or vast crowds of people. Maybe for you, seeing aerial photographs of the world, space or the stars and planets makes your heart soar.

Some people find their hearts lifted and their minds turned to God's beauty, majesty and love by nature, and some people find that human creativity or love or generosity does that for them more. So you might be moved to adore God by art, or by beautiful churches; a soaring cathedral spire; music, whether a soloist or a rock concert; pictures, stories or YouTube clips of charities working to relieve hunger and poverty and suffering.

Reminders of God's story in the Bible might also have this effect: from pictures of Jesus being born on Christmas cards, to statues or stained glass pictures of the crucifixion, or the empty tomb, or stories from the Bible. Hearing certain stories from the Bible, or worshipping in church with family and friends, or singing certain songs, might also move you to a sense of adoring God.

The experiment

FIRST, SPEND SOME TIME THINKING ABOUT WHAT MOVES YOU TO A SENSE OF AWE AND WONDER, MAYBE JOTTING DOWN SOME NOTES OR EVEN MAKING A MIND MAP.

Then find pictures that represent these things for you, and use them to make an adoration collage. There are two ways of doing this. To make an actual collage that you can put up on your wall, search for the pictures you need in old magazines, newspapers and catalogues. You could also print out images you have found searching online. If you need to, you could include words or phrases too. Try to find a mixture of pictures, some that make you feel awe, wonder or praise when you look at them, and some that remind you of aspects of God or of the stories in the Bible that you want to adore God for.

When you come to actually put the collage together, write 'I adore you, God, for . . .' or simply 'Adoration' in the middle, and then surround that with images that each make you feel awe, wonder, or love for God and for all that God has made and done.

Alternatively, you could make the whole collage electronically, searching for the images you want and making a digital collage. It would still be good to print it out at the end, but you could maybe also make a slideshow that you could share with friends, your church, or your youth group.

Finally, if you have a hard copy, stick it up on your wall so that it is a reminder for you of how amazing God is.

Feedback

WHEN I TRIED THIS EXPERIMENT, I FOUND ...

DOING THIS KIND OF PRAYER MADE ME FEEL ...

THE THING I LIKED BEST ABOUT IT WAS ...

THINGS I WOULD TRY CHANGING NEXT TIME:

MARKS OUT OF 10:

Noah's review: 7/10

I did this as a slideshow, because doing it electronically meant it was easier to find the pictures. Doing it as an actual collage might feel a bit babyish, though I suppose it might be fun to pretend to be a little kid again, cutting and sticking! I really enjoyed doing it on the computer, and it meant there was no limit to the pictures I could choose.

To think about what pictures I wanted to use I had to really think about 'what reminds me of God?' I thought about when I have felt a sense of the world being so much bigger than me, and what makes me happy.

I started off with pictures of mountains, because they are majestic, and I've done some hill walking with Scouts and really felt a sense of the majesty of God when we got to the top. I also had a space rocket launch, because going into space was a world breakthrough and still seems amazing. I had various other nature pictures, and I chose a picture of my cat because cats are the best thing ever so obviously God made them! I ended up with a photo of a Christmas tree. Christmas is something that's meant to remind you of God, but most people normally forget about the true meaning of Christmas. So having a Christmas tree rather than a more obvious religious picture made me think how amazing Christmas was, but also how easily God can be forgotten about.

Other experimenters' notes

10/10 – I did a collage of all the things I adore God for – my family, animals, my friends, all sorts of food, all the different colours, nature, hills and mountains. It made me reflect on those things a bit, because often I take them for granted. I thought about all the good things God's done for us, and all the good things he's made. I give this 10 out of 10 because you can keep it once you have made it, and then when you look at it again it reminds you to think about all the things to pray for. (Daisy, 13)

7/10 – I MADE A COLLAGE OF THINGS I FOUND BEAUTIFUL, OR COMPLEX, OR AMAZING. AT FIRST IT WAS QUITE HARD TO THINK OF THINGS, BUT I THINK THAT THE THINGS I CHOSE WERE THE THINGS THAT MOST MAKE ME THINK HOW AMAZING GOD IS.

IT WAS QUITE FUN MAKING THE COLLAGE AND THINKING OF THE PICTURES I COULD INCLUDE. (EMILY, 17)

9/10 – I made a digital collage by googling different landscapes around the world. Each landscape is unique and people have different needs as to where they live. I also looked at pictures of nature, and I thought about nature and how no tree is the same and also rainbows are never the same. I associate this with good because everything is unique. Next time I could explore other ways that God is amazing. (Emma, 11)

10/10 - First I made a digital collage (using Google Images), which I felt failed because I got distracted - I made a collage of all the things that make me happy rather than things that made me think about how great God is. I called it 'Adoration (stuff that makes me happy)'. So I had pictures of kittens, chocolate, goats and some lovely mountain scenery. One of the goat pictures I found had the caption 'Stop what you're doing and look at this happy goat instead', and I put that in the middle of my collage! After making the collage, Mum and I read the instructions again and thought maybe I should have done this differently. So then I thought of pictures like a big wave, mountains, flowers and cats. It slightly drew my attention to the 'Watch on the floor' metaphor that we did in RE, which is someone finding a watch on the floor. A watch couldn't just be there by chance, so someone must have made it. It goes on to say that the watch is the world, and couldn't be chance. This way of praying is helpful. (Hazel, 13)

2 CONFESSION

The two meanings of confession

'Confession' has two distinct meanings in Christianity. The first is the one you are probably most familiar with – owning up to what you've done wrong. Normally, this includes saying sorry, and promising to try not to do it again – though we all know that is a promise we often don't keep! Most church services include a 'confession'. This is a time when the whole church congregation says sorry to God for not living up to the standard of human life that the Bible and Jesus' life set out for us.

The second meaning is again 'owning up', but this time to our faith. This kind of confession means standing up for what we believe in. In many churches we literally stand up for what we believe in, as everyone stands in the church service to say a Creed (from the Latin word *credo*, meaning 'I believe'), or other statement of faith: a short summary of what the Church believes about God.

Confession is the second element of the ACTS pattern of prayer. In our personal prayers, the very fact that we are praying at all is a 'confession' of sorts. By the act of praying, we are 'confessing' – saying that we believe – that there is a God who hears and answers prayers. So in our personal prayers we don't very often say a formal 'statement of faith'. But for as long as people have been praying, owning up to what we've done wrong has been an important part of prayer.

Confessing to change the future

God, of course, already knows everything that we have done. So by owning up, we aren't letting God into a secret that we could otherwise keep to ourselves. It's not like telling your mum that it was you that broke that plate, when she thought it was probably the cat! But God seems to like us to admit what we are doing wrong. (Even if your mum knew perfectly well it was you that broke the plate, she is likely to be pleased with your honesty if you own up.)

If we don't own up to what we are doing wrong, we can't change it. For Christians, the key idea is 'repentance', which is not just about confessing our mistakes, but actively committing to turning away from them and living differently. If we think, or try to pretend, that there is nothing at all wrong with how we are living our lives, then we are saying we don't intend to change anything. Sometimes we don't want to own up to things that are wrong because we are ashamed or embarrassed. But if we make a practice of regularly admitting that everything isn't perfect, we can help ourselves to focus on what changes we'd like to see.

Even for those who wouldn't call themselves Christian, admitting where things are going wrong and committing yourself to changing is a really important part of life. For example, no athlete gets to the top of her game by deciding she is so good there is nothing she needs to work on. No musician becomes brilliant at his instrument by deciding he is the best in the orchestra so he will stop practising. The same applies to all of our lives.

It is important, when you confess as part of your private prayers, to remember that confession and God's forgiveness go together. One of the things that Christians believe about Jesus' death on the cross is that as he died, he took on himself any blame and guilt that we should have for anything we might do wrong. So Jesus' death guarantees that God has already forgiven us. We don't confess because otherwise God won't like us: God always loves us, whatever we have done.

(A health warning: Sometimes people find this hard to believe, and can get stuck at feeling guilty. If this happens to you, or you can't shake off a feeling that God didn't mean to forgive *you*, then please go and talk about this to someone you trust from church, perhaps your vicar or youth worker.)

The experiment

GET SOME STONES. THEY DON'T NEED TO BE ANYTHING SPECIAL,
JUST COLLECT THEM FROM A NEARBY GARDEN. HAVE AT LEAST
THREE, AND UP TO SAY SIX OR SEVEN. PUT A BOWL OF WATER
IN FRONT OF YOU, AND THE STONES IN A PILE.

Sit down, and pick up the first stone. You could just pick any stone,
or you might want to choose one that seems to represent the thing
you are confessing in some way. Perhaps it is jagged or broken, big or
small, dark or pale? As you hold it, think about one thing in your life
that is not as good as it could be. Own up to it. Then put the stone
into the water: you are giving it to God, not holding its weight any
longer. And it is being washed clean.

Pick up the next stone and think of something else in your life that
is not as good as it could be. Repeat as many times as seems right.
When you have finished, you might like to end by simply saying
'Amen', or you could repeat this traditional prayer: 'Lord, have mercy.
Christ, have mercy. Lord, have mercy.'

If you can't find stones easily, you could write down the things you
want to confess on pieces of paper, and watch them dissolve and
the writing blur as they sit in the water.

Feedback

WHEN I TRIED THIS EXPERIMENT, I FOUND . . .

DOING THIS KIND OF PRAYER MADE ME FEEL . . .

THE THING I LIKED BEST ABOUT IT WAS . . .

THINGS I WOULD TRY CHANGING NEXT TIME:

MARKS OUT OF 10:

Noah's review: 8/10

I quite enjoyed this. I found that looking closely at the stones and choosing ones that represented what I wanted to say was quite meaningful. So the first stone I picked was one I have on my desk anyway, that says 'joy' on it, and as I put that in the water I said sorry for not being as joyful as I could and should be.

For the second stone, I chose the smallest one I could find. That was because I often think of myself as quite big, more important than other people, which I know is wrong (and I'm sure this is not just me!). So I deliberately chose a small stone to acknowledge that I'm really quite small compared to the rest of creation. Then I had a stone that was quite rough, to say sorry for when I take my anger out on other people, like my younger brother. And the last one was for not trying as hard as I could at things.

Putting them in the water was also effective. There wasn't actually that much water in the bowl I had, so the bigger ones I had to turn over so they got wet all over. Physically doing that gave me a real sense of helping God wash them, it felt like it showed I knew those things were wrong and was volunteering to have them washed away.

Other experimenters' notes

10/10 – I just used one stone, and I thought it was quite effective. Because it was heavy and cold, it was a good way of imagining your sins or the things that are wrong.

Then putting it in the water was like washing your sins clean. I really liked that. Plus it made quite an effective sound when it hit the bottom! It made a loud clunk, so it made you think again that the sins were heavy but that you'd let them go and they'd fallen to the bottom of the water.

When I was doing it with a group we used a clear bowl, and we had some candles lit behind it. That was good because you could see the water, and see the stones being washed. It made the water look really pure, and the candlelight shone through it and was reflected in it, which seemed to emphasize the water's meaning. We discussed whether it would work better or differently if you used a dark bowl and coloured the water black, so the stones would completely disappear in the depths, but I liked the clear water. (Emily, 17)

7/10 – THIS WORKED REALLY WELL. I LIKED THE IDEA OF VISUALIZING THE THINGS THAT WERE BOTHERING YOU, AND PUTTING THEM INTO THE STONES. TO BE HONEST, I WASN'T VERY SURE THAT THE WATER WAS NEEDED. IT WOULD HAVE WORKED FINE JUST PUTTING THE STONES DOWN, JUST LETTING GO OF THEM. (LUKE, 16)

10/10 – Top marks for effectiveness, using paper that we wrote things on instead of stones. (Blackburn Cathedral confirmation group)

10/10

- Extremely peaceful.
- It was nice to think what we need to own up to.
- Very reflective.
- We ended up discussing why confession is important, and whether you can confess something which you don't think you can do anything to change.

(Members of 'Encounter', All Saints Church, High Wycombe)

3 THANKSGIVING

More than politeness

Do you remember being given things when you were younger?
Birthday and Christmas presents, or a share in someone else's sweets?
If so, you can probably also remember parents or teachers hissing to
you 'Say thank you!' Saying please and thank you is a basic element
of the politeness that is dinned into us as children.

But strangely enough, having learnt to be polite can be a problem
when it comes to prayers of thankfulness. We don't say thank you to
God for quite the same reasons as we thank other people. We don't
say thank you to God just to be polite, or to make God feel better!
We say thank you to God mainly because of what that does to us.
Saying thank you means that we are doing two important things:

1. We are choosing to look at the good things in our lives with
    gratitude, not just focus on things that aren't right; and

2. We are acknowledging that everything we have comes from God.

Let's look at what each of those means in a bit more detail. First,
we are choosing to concentrate on the good. There is an old saying,
'Count your blessings', and it is generally true that if we focus on
the good things in life rather than the bad, we are likely to be much
happier. Focusing on the positive doesn't mean ignoring the bad
things in life – after all, sometimes things are seriously wrong and

need to be challenged. But even in some of the worst situations there are likely to be some good things that we can give thanks to God for.

Second, when we thank God for all the good things we have received, we are acknowledging that everything comes from God. This is important for at least two reasons. It means we are recognizing God as the Creator, the basic source of everything, from the Big Bang onwards. So thanking God is a statement of faith. It also means recognizing that all the good things we have are not ours by right, but are gifts. Even the things that we ourselves have achieved or have earned, we are only able to do because of the gifts of character, talent and aptitude that we are born with, and because of the circumstances in which we are born. How much would we be able to achieve if we had been born several hundred years ago, or not had an education?

So thanking God means both recognizing ourselves as gifted people, and cultivating a sense of humility. In thanking God for our gifts we gradually come to see ourselves as someone that God loves and showers with gifts, but also as no more special or loved by God than anyone else.

The experiment

BECAUSE IT MEANS ALL THIS, SAYING THANK YOU TO GOD IS AN IMPORTANT PART OF THE CHRISTIAN TRADITION OF PRAYER. BUT IT CAN OFTEN BECOME QUITE REPETITIVE AND BORING. PEOPLE OFTEN FIND THAT WHEN IT COMES TO SAYING THANK YOU, THEIR MIND GOES BLANK! OR WE REPEAT OURSELVES, SAYING THANK YOU TO GOD FOR THE SAME, OBVIOUS THINGS EVERY TIME WE PRAY.

To help focus your prayers of thanksgiving, try making a Jar of Thankfulness.

1. Get an empty, clean jam jar with the label removed – or some other pot or bowl.

2. Cut some paper into strips. (Coloured paper works well if you're using a glass jar.)

3. On each strip of paper, write one thing that you are thankful for, and add the strips to the jar. Keep a spare supply of pieces of paper next to the jar, and whenever you think of something new to say thanks for, add it to the jar.

4. Once you have your Jar of Thankfulness, keep it somewhere safe where you will see it regularly – perhaps on your windowsill or bedside table, or in a prayer corner with any other prayer items

that you may have. When you sit down to pray, take a handful of the contents out and say thank you for those, adding any new ones that you have thought of that day to the jar. Doing this will mean you keep some variety in your prayers, and also slowly build up a collection of more and more things to be thankful for.

Feedback

WHEN I TRIED THIS EXPERIMENT, I FOUND . . .

DOING THIS KIND OF PRAYER MADE ME FEEL . . .

THE THING I LIKED BEST ABOUT IT WAS . . .

THINGS I WOULD TRY CHANGING NEXT TIME:

MARKS OUT OF 10:

Noah's review: 8/10

I made smallish paper strips and wrote down things I was thankful for. I folded them up and put them into the jar and put it on my bedside cabinet. I took one out that evening and prayed for it just before going to bed.

Then the next day when I came to pray with it I wrote a couple more and added them to the jar. Then I took a handful out to pray with. When I unfolded them, the three that I had picked turned out to be 'thank you for keeping me safe from conflicts', 'thank you for my loving family' and 'thank you that I live a happy life'. I prayed for those one at a time, as I opened them — first saying thank you for that thing, and then praying for people who weren't as lucky as me or didn't have that particular thing.

Having a sort of lucky dip like this meant that I didn't have to think what to pray for. Normally when I pray I find I pray for quite generic things, so having this meant I prayed not just for the normal things but for the things I was given. I thought that was a really good idea and I will keep using it. I might remove some of the strips if I find I have prayed for them a lot, as well as adding new ones as they occur to me.

I think you could extend this jar idea and have two jars, one of things to say thank you for and one of things to ask God for. I might do that, and use different colour paper for each one.

Other experimenters' notes

9/10 – I decorated a jar with shiny paper and wrote ten thank yous on coloured paper. I placed this on my windowsill in my bedroom. When I tried this experiment it made me feel sorry for other people that did not have what I have. It made me feel more aware of people without food or water. I liked having a written reminder of my thank yous. (Emma, 11)

7/10 – I GOT A SHEET OF PAPER AND PENS AND WROTE DOWN WHAT I WAS THANKFUL FOR, THEN CUT IT UP INTO SMALL STRIPS AND FOLDED THEM UP AND PUT THEM IN A SMALL JAR. THE SORT OF THINGS I WROTE DOWN WERE MY FRIENDS, FAMILY, THE INTERNET BECAUSE IT ALLOWS ME TO CONTACT PEOPLE, AND THE GIFT OF LAUGHTER BECAUSE I ENJOY LAUGHING, IT MAKES ME HAPPY. I HAD ABOUT 15 OR 20 THINGS IN TOTAL.

ONCE I HAD CUT THEM UP, AS I FOLDED EACH ONE UP AND PUT IT INTO THE JAR I SAID THANK YOU TO GOD FOR IT, AND ASKED GOD TO GIVE ME MORE OF THAT THING OR TO KEEP IT SAFE. I HAVEN'T BEEN ADDING TO THE JAR, THOUGH I SUPPOSE I MIGHT IN THE FUTURE IF SOMETHING NEW HAPPENS. I AM NOW KEEPING THE JAR ON THE TABLE BY MY BED, AND WHEN I SEE IT, IT REMINDS ME OF ALL THE THINGS IN MY LIFE THAT ARE GOOD. (REUBEN, 13)

8/10 – I did this with a friend, and we started off by brainstorming what we were thankful for, and writing it all down on strips of paper to go in the jar. Some of mine were: 'I'm thankful for music', 'I'm thankful for family', 'I'm thankful for the air to breathe', 'I'm thankful for my senses', 'I'm thankful for acceptance'.

I felt quite inspired and grateful as I was coming up with the things to write down.

When we'd made the jars, we put them by our beds, and I have found since then that whenever I see it – which of course is several times a day – it makes me feel really thankful. Even without opening it up and reading the bits of paper, just seeing it there reminds me of all the things I thought of.

I like the idea of adding to it as I think of more things, and I would definitely recommend other people to try making one of these. It made me feel really grateful and thankful. (Jasmine, 14)

4 SUPPLICATION

Supplication (also known as asking or intercession) is the final element of the ACTS four-part balanced diet of prayer. This is probably the kind of prayer that you are most familiar with. For many people, praying mainly means asking God to do things, to look after people, and to intervene in difficult situations.

In most church services, there is a time of Intercessory Prayer when the concerns of the congregation are lifted up to God. Typically these include prayers for the Church, the world, the suffering, and those who have died or are dying and their families. These prayers are often referred to simply as 'The Prayers', when they are in fact just one of the many kinds of prayer that are used in the service.

Asking God for what you want

Sometimes, this kind of praying is criticized or looked down on, as if it was just about sending a wish list to a kind of cosmic Father Christmas. But although *just* asking God for things would be a very limited kind of praying, asking God is something that Jesus told people to do. For example, one of the parables (stories with a message) that Jesus told was the parable of the persistent widow:

> In a certain city there was a judge who neither feared God nor had respect for people. In that city there was a widow who kept coming to him and saying, 'Grant me justice against my opponent.' For a while he refused; but later he said to himself, 'Though I have no fear of God and no respect for anyone, yet because this widow keeps bothering me, I will grant her justice, so that she may not wear me out by continually coming.' And the Lord said, 'Listen to what the unjust judge says. And will not God grant justice to his chosen ones who cry to him day and night?' (Luke 18.2–7)

Jesus also included the line 'give us today our daily bread' in the Lord's Prayer, the prayer he taught his disciples when they asked him to teach them how to pray.

So, far from being embarrassed to ask God for the things we need and desire, we should make sure we regularly include an element of asking in our prayers.

As with thanksgiving, asking God to help means a lot more than just what it seems on the surface. In no particular order:

● It means admitting that we can't achieve everything we want to happen by ourselves. Very often there are situations around the world, and closer to home, that make us feel helpless. We feel powerless to make a difference, and yet we feel very strongly that something must be done. In asking God's help, we are acknowledging the limits of our own influence.

● We are also, though, opening ourselves up to the possibility that we may have to do something to be part of the solution.

In asking God to help in a situation, it is always worth listening for a while after asking, in case you hear something that you can do. In this kind of prayer we consciously volunteer ourselves as God's assistants or co-workers in bringing about change.

- Supplication is also a confession of faith in God. By asking God to intervene in a situation, we are saying we believe that God has the power to do so. This doesn't mean we expect miracles to happen every time we pray, but it does mean we are opening our minds to the possibility of God's transforming power making a difference in the world. Regularly asking for God's help cultivates an attitude of hopeful expectancy in us.

What to ask for

It is OK to ask for anything that is on your mind! The Bible is full of examples of people asking for what they most want, from good things like food, water and justice, to bad things like revenge.

Basically, the rule of thumb is to be honest. Tell God what you are really feeling, what you are desperate about, what you want more than anything in the world. The Christian belief is that God knows what you are thinking anyway, of course, so you might as well be honest! God isn't going to think any better of you for trying to hide your true feelings and desires. And you can trust God to know if something you are asking for would be really bad for you or for other people, and to do what is the most loving thing.

We know from the Bible that God can intervene in the world to change things, but also that it is quite unusual for miracles to happen. So it is worth praying for things that seem impossible, but be prepared for your prayers to be answered in ways other than what you expected or were hoping for. For example, not everyone we pray for who is ill will get better – everyone dies at some time – but even then we can trust that God will hear our prayers and help them to die at peace and be with God in heaven after they die, and comfort those who mourn.

The experiment

TO HELP YOU THINK MORE CLEARLY ABOUT WHAT THINGS TO
ASK GOD FOR, TRY MAKING A PRAYER TREE.

1. Gather some twigs, and put them in a vase or empty jam jar;
   or you could use a fairly substantial potted plant for this, or
   even a jewellery tree.

2. Now get some little notes to hang on the twigs. The
   easiest thing is to use gift tags with a hanging loop
   of thread already attached. Or just use pieces of
   paper, either plain or cut out to look like leaves.
   If you do that, use a hole punch or a sharp pencil
   to make a hole in each one, and pass through a loop
   of thread, wool or gift ribbon so it can be hung on
   the tree.

3. Write each situation, or the name of each person,
   that you want to ask God's help for on one of the tags,
   and hang it on the tree, consciously giving that situation
   or person to God and handing over your worry about it to
   God as you do so. Then place the tree somewhere in your
   room.

You might want to sit and pray through each of the tags
every day, or once a week, and you can add new ones
whenever you like. When one no longer needs praying

for, you can remove it from the tree. You might want to keep any prayers that you feel have been answered in a box: if you keep adding to the tree regularly, then this box could become a lovely record of answered prayers.

Feedback

WHEN I TRIED THIS EXPERIMENT, I FOUND ...

DOING THIS KIND OF PRAYER MADE ME FEEL ...

THE THING I LIKED BEST ABOUT IT WAS ...

THINGS I WOULD TRY CHANGING NEXT TIME:

MARKS OUT OF 10:

Noah's review: 9/10

I thought this was really good because of the interactivity of going and getting the sticks and actually making the tree. That made it feel more personal. If I did it again I would put more prayerful thought into actually making the tree. The concept of a tree is giving people life, because trees give out oxygen, so making a prayer tree to pray for people linked together really well.

I made little tags, hole punched them and hung them on the tree with bits of wool. On each one I drew a picture, or cut it into a particular shape, to symbolize what I was praying for, and then wrote on the other side. One of them was for a recent disaster, for example, and I drew a picture to symbolize that, and then wrote on the back that I was praying for the people who had lost their families. Another one I cut into the shape of a leaf, and I used that to pray for my siblings.

Putting the prayers onto the tree it felt a bit like I was actually giving the people life and hope. It felt as if God was somehow in the tree, looking at the people I was putting on it and praying with me for them.

Other experimenters' notes

9/10 – I used a small tree growing in a pot, and some small Post-It notes for this experiment. I wrote the prayers on the Post-It notes and stuck them on the leaves of the tree. I had the idea in my head that when the Post-It notes fell off the tree, that would mean that the prayer had been answered.

I liked this because it allowed me to write down things that I needed or wanted to happen and it was fun at the same time. I couldn't think of what to pray for at first, but then I prayed for stopping a war that's in the news a lot at the moment, and providing food for the poor who need it.

I felt my prayers were being listened to by God. When I do this again I might use twigs, thread or parcel tags to hang the prayers on the tree. They wouldn't fall off, but when I felt my prayers had been answered I would take them off. (Daniel, 11)

2/10 – I TRIED MAKING A PRAYER TREE AND IT DID NOT WORK VERY WELL. FIRST, IT HAD JUST RAINED (A LOT) SO THAT WHEN I EVENTUALLY FOUND THEM, THE STICKS WERE SOGGY. THE SOIL IN THE POT ALSO STUCK TOGETHER, MAKING IT HARD TO PUT THE STICKS IN. WHEN IT WAS FINALLY FINISHED, I FOUND IT DIDN'T REALLY HELP ME TO PRAY, AS I WAS DISTRACTED BY HAVING A LUMP OF MUD IN FRONT OF ME. (CALLUM, 15)

9.5/10 – This was one of my favourite activities. I liked the fact that it was so interactive – I went and collected twigs and put them in a jar, and then I cut out leaf shapes to hang on the twigs. So I thought it was especially good for creative people. I decided to make my prayer tags in the shape of leaves, because I could make it more interesting with all the different leaf shapes, it was fun decorating them, and it looks really pretty. I prayed for things like wars, and for individual people that I know who are going through hardship.

The idea of a prayer tree was interesting because it was related to nature and gave you a lot of freedom in what you could do, and it was fun to create. Making the individual leaves helped me focus on the things I was praying for, and stopped me going off on tangents.

I will do this again, and probably put on more leaves next time. I might use the news to help me think of things to include. (Jasmine, 14)

The Lord's Prayer

The prayer that Jesus taught

If you find praying difficult, you might be reassured to know that even the first disciples didn't really know what to do! One of the things that they found strangest about Jesus was that he regularly went off on his own to pray (see, for example, Mark 1.35–37).

The disciples asked Jesus to teach them how to pray, and he taught them the short form of the prayer that we now call 'The Lord's Prayer'. There are slightly different versions of it in different accounts (you can look them up: Matthew 5.9–13 and Luke 11.1–4). The versions we use today vary slightly between churches, but all are similar.

> **Our Father in heaven,**
> **Hallowed be your name.**
> **Your kingdom come,**
> **Your will be done,**
> **On earth as it is in heaven.**
> **Give us today our daily bread,**
> **And forgive us our sins,**
> **As we forgive those who sin against us.**
> **And lead us not into temptation,**
> **But deliver us from evil.**
> **For the kingdom, the power and the glory are yours**
> **For ever and ever.**
> **Amen.**

Using the Lord's Prayer

What is not known is how Jesus meant these words to be used. Did he mean 'say exactly these words'? Or did he mean 'include these topics when you pray'? We don't know. But we say the Lord's Prayer in almost every church service, and many Christians use it every day as part of their own prayers. It used to be the first prayer that children were taught, and one of the things you had to be able to recite to be considered a Christian.

Simply saying the Lord's Prayer – reciting the familiar words – is a good way to start or end prayers, and saying it every day is a good idea. Doing this is very reassuring if you aren't sure what to say, because you know that you are doing what Jesus told his followers to do.

The experiment

ANOTHER WAY TO USE THE LORD'S PRAYER IS TO THINK OF IT AS A SERIES OF HEADINGS, OR BULLET POINTS, TO MAKE SURE THAT YOU HAVE COVERED ALL THE IMPORTANT SUBJECTS IN YOUR PRAYERS. GO THROUGH IT SLOWLY, PHRASE BY PHRASE. AS YOU DO SO, THINK ABOUT WHAT EACH PHRASE MEANS, AND

PRAY FOR WHAT IT MEANS IN YOUR LIFE, OR FOR THINGS YOU ARE WORRIED ABOUT AT THE MOMENT. SPEND A MINUTE OR TWO THINKING ABOUT EACH LINE AND WHAT IT MEANS FOR YOU. DON'T WORRY IF SOME LINES MEAN MORE TO YOU THAN OTHERS. YOU MIGHT WANT TO WRITE THE PRAYER OUT AGAIN VERY SLOWLY, OR REWRITE IT IN YOUR OWN WORDS, OR SIMPLY NOTE DOWN SOMETHING ABOUT WHAT EACH LINE MEANS TO YOU PERSONALLY. OR YOU COULD TRY WRITING IT OUT DECORATIVELY, AND REALLY THINKING ABOUT WHAT COLOUR, STYLE OR DECORATION TO USE FOR EACH PART OF IT TO REFLECT WHAT IT MEANS.

Here are some ideas about each phrase to start you thinking.

Our Father in heaven

If God is our father – our creator, and someone who loves and cares for us – what does that mean? And what does it mean for our relationship with other people, if God is their father too?

Hallowed be your name

This means 'may everyone call you holy'. This is about recognizing that God is totally pure, goodness, truth, light and life: it isn't just any person we call our father, but the God who is totally holy and yet loves us and wants us to love him.

Your kingdom come

What do you hope would be different about life in God's kingdom?

Your will be done

This part of the prayer says 'I want all the things I am asking for, but I accept it is up to you whether I get them. I believe you know what is best for me and everyone and I trust you.' It also reminds us of Jesus praying in the Garden of Gethsemane the night before he was killed, accepting whatever God's will for him was (Luke 22.39–46).

On earth as it is in heaven

This means that we don't just aim to get through life and look forward to a better life afterwards: we want to work with

God to make this world a better place. How might you be called to help that come about?

79

Give us today our daily bread

Here we are asking for what we need, but not for everything we would like: we are only asking for enough for today. So we are trusting God one day at a time, and trying not to worry too much about the future. This can be really difficult, and that's OK. But saying these words reminds us gently to try to worry about just one day at a time.

Forgive us our sins

We might not feel we have 'sins', as it sounds quite heavy and serious. But Jesus included these words for everyone. Saying them means we are admitting to God that we are not perfect. We are both asking that God will show us how we could be better people, and trusting that our faults never stop God loving us and hearing our prayers.

As we forgive those who sin against us

People often misunderstand what this means. Forgiving doesn't mean forgetting. For example, you can forgive your brother for breaking your stuff without having to let him carry on playing with it. You can forgive someone who has let you down or hurt you, but you might be sensible to think twice before you trust them again. I think 'forgiving' means something like 'letting go'. If you are angry with someone, it can feel like letting them off if you choose to stop being angry. But Christians believe – and scientists agree – that choosing not to hold on to anger makes you a happier and healthier person.

80

Lead us not into temptation

This and the next line are both asking for bad things not to happen. 'Temptation' is when we feel we want to do something that we know is wrong. This line asks that we will be protected from finding ourselves in situations where we will have to make difficult decisions, or where we will be tempted to do something that will hurt ourselves or others. In the privacy of your own prayers, ask yourself honestly: when are you tempted to do wrong things?

Deliver us from evil

This line is a catch-all prayer asking for protection from bad or scary things. Evil will mean different things to you: illness, people dying, people wanting to hurt us. And maybe also, asking for help for us not to be evil to other people?

For the kingdom, the power and the glory are yours for ever and ever. Amen

This isn't part of the original prayer that the Bible records Jesus teaching the disciples, but is a way of rounding off the prayer when we use it. It is also a statement of faith that because God is the same for ever, everything that Jesus showed us about God is still true. So we can pray all this trusting that God loves us, and has the power to help us.

'Amen' simply means 'Let it be so'.

81

OUR FATHER IN HEAVEN

HALLOWED BE YOUR NAME

YOUR KINGDOM COME

YOUR WILL BE DONE

ON EARTH AS IT IS IN HEAVEN

GIVE US TODAY OUR DAILY BREAD

AND FORGIVE US OUR SINS

AS WE FORGIVE THOSE WHO SIN AGAINST US

AND LEAD US NOT INTO TEMPTATION

BUT DELIVER US FROM EVIL

FOR THE KINGDOM, THE POWER AND THE GLORY ARE YOURS

FOR EVER AND EVER. AMEN.

Feedback

THE THING I LIKED BEST ABOUT PRAYING LIKE THIS WAS . . .

THINGS I WOULD TRY CHANGING NEXT TIME:

MARKS OUT OF 10:

Noah's review: 5/10

This was a bit too wordy for me. But writing my response to each line did help me to think about what the prayer really means.

It's a very familiar prayer, I know it off by heart from school and church, so I wasn't expecting much from going through it yet again. But when I was writing what each line meant to me I did find I specially noticed the line 'Give us today our daily bread'. Noticing that made me think quite a lot about what it meant. It can't refer to communion, which was my thought when I was younger, because that is normally just on Sunday, not 'daily'. So daily bread must mean something else. If God is giving us bread, and at the time Jesus first said this prayer that was the main food, the main life source, that's like God keeping us going every day. So I realized this wasn't just about literally asking for food, but for God to sustain us and keep us alive day by day.

Then that made me think, well God doesn't decide everything we do. We have been given the ability to make decisions, and so I suddenly thought of this prayer being partly about asking God to help us make the right decisions every day as well.

So it did make me think, but I didn't find it a particularly engaging way of praying.

Other experimenters' notes

10/10 – This was nice, because it makes you think about it a lot. The notes gave me quite a lot to work on. I wrote the prayer out in nice writing and put it up decoratively, and it made me think about what the individual words mean and what the prayer means as whole. To a lot of people it's just a prayer that you say, and I found that trying to figure it out means I can say it with more meaning now.

The words 'Our father in heaven' are so familiar but they jumped out: we call God Father, so it shows us he wants us to have a close relationship with him.

If you do this, I'd say to look out for particular words and then work out what the rest of the sentence means from that key word. (Catherine, 15)

7/10 – I JUST COLOURED IN AROUND THE WORDS IN DIFFERENT COLOURS, WHICH ALLOWED ME TO THINK ABOUT WHY THOSE WORDS HAD BEEN CHOSEN.

I CHOSE RED FOR WORDS LIKE SIN BECAUSE I ASSOCIATED RED AND SIN WITH THE DEVIL. I USED BLUE AND GREEN AS COLOURS FOR PURITY FOR THE WORDS THAT HAD A LINK TO GOD, BECAUSE GOD CREATED THE WORLD, THE WATER AND LAND AND EVERYTHING FOR THAT MATTER.

I THOUGHT IT WAS QUITE A NICE IDEA BECAUSE IT ALLOWS YOU TO FOCUS ON THE PRAYER A LOT AND I THOUGHT IT ALLOWED ME TO CONNECT WITH GOD. (DANIEL, 11)

Colouring
the
Bible

Letting the Bible speak to you

One of the oldest forms of prayer in the Christian tradition is reading the Bible. It might not sound much like prayer to you, as nowadays we often think of prayer as just being what we do when we are sitting quietly with our eyes closed, asking God for things. You might be more used to thinking of the Bible as something you read for information, or instruction. But reading the Bible prayerfully is a very important strand of the Christian spiritual tradition.

One way that Christians sometimes use the Bible in praying is to focus on a short passage and stay with it for quite a long time. Sometimes people say that when they read a Bible passage once, or even twice through, it stays as just words on a page. But when you've read it three or four times, suddenly something about it might jump out at you, or you hear it differently.

This is what people mean when they say the Bible 'spoke' to them: suddenly, a word, or a phrase, jumped out at them and seemed to mean something specific for them. Or they suddenly saw something different about a story they'd heard many times before, and understood something new about it. You might find you suddenly see a similarity between something happening in the passage and something going on in your own life, or feel that one particular word or phrase is what God wants to say to you just at this moment. This doesn't always happen dramatically, but if you read and meditate on a passage several times and stay with it long enough, you will almost always find that something about it seems new to you by the end.

Illuminated manuscripts

One way of staying with a passage long enough for it to speak to you is to decorate it, or colour the words in. When medieval monks were copying out the Bible by hand, before printing was invented, they would often decorate some letters and words very elaborately. Illuminated manuscripts are beautiful for us to look at, but the idea behind doing this wasn't only to make them look pretty. Decorating individual letters and words meant that the scribe spent more time contemplating the words. It also meant that anyone reading it was likely to spend more time looking at it and appreciating it.

The experiment

TRY MAKING YOUR OWN ILLUMINATED MANUSCRIPT. AS YOU ARE COLOURING IN THE WORDS AND IMAGES, YOU WILL BE ABLE TO THINK ABOUT THEM FOR QUITE A LONG TIME. AND THE FACT THAT YOU ARE CONCENTRATING ON COLOURING IN MEANS YOU WON'T BE TOO FOCUSED ON THE WORDS: YOUR CONSCIOUS MIND WILL BE OCCUPIED, LEAVING YOUR SUBCONSCIOUS TO MEDITATE ON THE PASSAGE WITHOUT THINKING ABOUT IT TOO MUCH.

If you would prefer to make your own illumination, first choose a passage that is just a sentence or two long – you could ask someone to suggest one for you, or you might remember a story from school or from hearing it in church, or you can find one by just flicking through the Bible. Enjoy deciding the best way to lay it out on the page, what style of writing fits it best, how you might illustrate it. Use the whole page, decorate every centimetre, take at least half an hour and make it as beautiful or dramatic as you can. It probably works best if you make the writing, or at least some of the letters, hollow (like bubble writing), so that you can first draw the outlines of the words, and then colour them in. That way you will spend longer with each word, rather than just quickly writing out the passage and spending the time decorating round the edge of it. Make the words the stars of the show.

You don't have to draw your own: if you prefer to colour in a version that someone else has drawn then there are various books and print-out sheets available. You can buy some lovely – and very elaborate –

books of Bible passages to colour in from The Lindisfarne Scriptorium (available online at <www.lindisfarne-scriptorium.co.uk>). There are also several available free online, for example at the Flame Creative website (<www.flamecreativekids.blogspot.co.uk>, under 'Creative prayer' and then 'Reflective colouring'): just find one you like the look of and print it out, or use the one provided on pages 92–3, which is from Flame Creative.

Another way of doing this would be to make a cartoon strip or comic book version of the part of the Bible you have chosen. Try to spend plenty of time over this. Rather than doing a passage that is full of action, try choosing a slower passage, full of interesting imagery, so that you have to think more about how to draw it. You could try a psalm, for example. And again, try to pay at least as much attention to the lettering as to the illustration, so that you are spending a lot of time with the words themselves. As a real challenge, try doing one frame of the cartoon strip for every word or phrase of the passage, rather than summing up a sentence or two in each frame.

The grace of our Lord Jesus Christ and the love of God and the

Fellowship of
the Holy Spirit
be with us all
evermore.
Amen

AMW 2014

Feedback

WHEN I TRIED THIS EXPERIMENT, I FOUND . . .

SPENDING TIME WITH THESE WORDS, I FELT . . .

THE THING I LIKED BEST ABOUT IT WAS . . .

THINGS I WOULD TRY CHANGING NEXT TIME:

MARKS OUT OF 10:

Noah's review: 6/10

I enjoyed doing this, it was really fun. The picture I was doing (from the Flame Creative Kids website) did not make me think about the Bible passage that was written on it – 'For God so loved the world that he gave his only Son, so that everyone who believes in him may not be lost but may have eternal life' (John 3.16) – but it did make me think about the picture itself.

The picture had a hand, with a sort of rainbow pathway coming out of it. A hand to me means feel or touch so the hand, to me, meant God feels for us with his whole heart. The sort of rainbow pathway indicates the pathway to God's love, heaven.

I like colouring in, but to me this wasn't really a prayer experience.

I think part of the problem might have been that this was a Bible passage I know well, and I've done some Ethics and Philosophy work on it at school. When I tried it again, using a passage I was given that I didn't know so well, it was much more meaningful and really made me think about the words.

Other experimenters' notes

8/10 – I found that doing this really made the passage speak to me. It made me feel that God could really speak to me through his word, and it was a good way to help me focus on what God was saying. It might be an improvement next time to have a small space on the page to just draw anything God gave to you. (Jonny, 14)

8/10 – I COLOURED IN THE LORD'S PRAYER. IT REALLY HELPED ME CONCENTRATE ON WHAT EACH WORD MEANT AS I COLOURED THEM AND IT ALSO HELPS TO LINK THE LORD'S PRAYER INTO MY OWN LIFE. (SAMANTHA, 16)

7/10 – When I tried this experiment I found that it was good fun, but I still felt that the prayer was sinking in and it made me think of it in a new way. It made me feel relaxed. The thing I liked best was the simpleness of it. Next time I would try using a more memorable quotation, with less of the background image and more focus on just the words. (Rachel, 15)

Lego
Bible
modelling

Spending time in the Bible

The idea of spending time immersing yourself in the Scriptures is even older than Christianity. The Psalms from the Jewish Scriptures, our Old Testament, talk a lot about the practice of meditating on God's law. Reading, praying with and thinking about the Scriptures is described as being like a tree, with our roots going deep into the life-giving soil, drinking up the life-giving water. If we meditate on what is written we become deeply rooted, fed, stable and fruitful.

Meditating on the Bible doesn't have to mean always agreeing with it. Reading the Bible prayerfully is not about deciding whether it is true or not, or doing what it says. It is simply about spending time with the stories there, and seeing what they say to us about God, about the world, and about ourselves.

One famous way of using the Bible for prayer is called the 'Ignatian' method, because it was invented in medieval times by St Ignatius. The idea is that you read a Bible story, usually an episode from the Gospels, and imagine yourself there.

What does it feel like (hot? Cold? Windy? Sandy?), smell like (dirty people? Camels? Flowers? Blood? Water?), sound like (is it busy? Shouting? Silence? Birdsong?), and so on.

Then you imagine yourself in the scene. Who is there? What about you yourself – what part are you playing? Are you a bystander, or one of the characters in the scene? And then you imagine Jesus turning to you. What does he say?

The experiment

THIS IS A BIT LIKE THAT, BUT LESS 'SIT STILL AND THINK' AND MORE 'GET OUT THE LEGO AND BUILD'. YOU ARE GOING TO RECREATE, IN LEGO, A STORY FROM THE BIBLE. THE CHALLENGE ISN'T JUST TO WORK OUT WHAT THE SCENE WOULD HAVE LOOKED LIKE. YOU'LL ALSO NEED TO THINK ABOUT WHAT THE CHARACTERS ARE THINKING OR FEELING AT DIFFERENT POINTS IN THE STORY. TRY TO CHOOSE LEGO FIGURES WITH APPROPRIATE FACIAL EXPRESSIONS, AND POSE THEM IN WAYS THAT EXPRESS WHAT YOU THINK THEY ARE FEELING.

The first thing you'll need to do is choose a Bible story. There are some suggested below, but you can choose something else if you prefer, maybe one of the readings you have heard in church or assembly recently. Or you could ask a parent or youth leader or minister to suggest one for you. If you have a group of friends to do this with, it can be fun to all try the same story and see how different your models are.

You can decide whether you want to model the whole story, or just one scene from it. If you want to model the whole thing, you could try taking a series of photographs of the different scenes as you go, and create a sort of photo cartoon strip. You could even take lots of photos and try putting them into some stop-motion animation software, to make a short animation of the story. If you do this, why not offer it to school or your local church for them to show in assembly or a service, instead of just reading the story?

When you have finished, you could show your model, or photographs, to friends and family, compare your version with your friends' and discuss the differences, put the pictures on Facebook or tweet them.

Some suggestions for stories that other people have enjoyed modelling

Jesus calms the storm (in the Bible at Matthew 8.23–27)

When Jesus got into the boat, his disciples followed him. A gale arose on the lake, so great that the boat was being swamped by the waves; but he was asleep. And they went and woke him up, saying, 'Lord, save us! We are perishing!' And he said to them, 'Why are you afraid, you of little faith?' Then he got up and rebuked the winds and the sea; and there was a dead calm. They were amazed, saying, 'What sort of man is this, that even the winds and the sea obey him?'

Jesus anointed with perfume (in the Bible at Mark 14.3–9)

While Jesus was at Bethany in the house of Simon the leper, as he sat at the table, a woman came with an alabaster jar of very costly ointment of nard, and she broke open the jar and poured the ointment on his head. But some were there who said to one another in anger, 'Why was the ointment wasted in this way? For this ointment could have been sold for more than three hundred denarii, and the money given to the poor.' And they scolded her. But Jesus said, 'Let her alone; why do you trouble her? She has performed a good service for me. For you always have the poor with you, and you can show kindness to them whenever you wish; but you will not always have me. She has done what she could; she has anointed my body beforehand for its burial. Truly I tell you, wherever the good news is proclaimed in the whole world, what she has done will be told in remembrance of her.'

The parable of the Good Samaritan (in the Bible at Luke 10.30–35)

Jesus replied, 'A man was going down from Jerusalem to Jericho, and fell into the hands of robbers, who stripped him, beat him, and went away, leaving him half dead. Now by chance a priest was going down that road; and when he saw him, he passed by on the other side. So likewise a Levite, when he came to the place and saw him, passed by on the other side. But a Samaritan while travelling came near him; and when he saw him, he was moved with pity. He went to him and bandaged his wounds, having poured oil and wine on them. Then he put him on his own animal, brought him to an inn, and took care of him. The next day he took out two denarii, gave them to the innkeeper, and said, 'Take care of him; and when I come back, I will repay you for whatever more you spend.'

Jesus appears to his disciples after the resurrection (in the Bible at John 20.19–22)

When it was evening on that day, the first day of the week, and the doors of the house where the disciples had met were locked for fear of the Jews, Jesus came and stood among them and said, 'Peace be with you.' After he said this, he showed them his hands and his side. Then the disciples rejoiced when they saw the Lord. Jesus said to them again, 'Peace be with you. As the Father has sent me, so I send you.' When he had said this, he breathed on them and said to them, 'Receive the Holy Spirit.'

Feedback

WHEN I TRIED THIS EXPERIMENT . . .

MODELLING THE BIBLE STORY MADE ME NOTICE . . .

THE THING I LIKED BEST ABOUT IT WAS . . .

THINGS I WOULD TRY CHANGING NEXT TIME:

MARKS OUT OF 10:

Noah's review: 8.5/10

I made a series of models of the story of the Good Samaritan. As soo
as I saw the story I had an idea in mind of what I was going to build.

I built the scene where the man gets attacked. I found some rocks
and had the robbers hiding behind those, and the man walking down
the road. I made sure I found Lego people with aggressive faces
to be the robbers, and I had them jump out from behind the rocks.
We took photos of the scene, and I got them jumping out by having
them dangling above the scene on threads while I took the photos.
Then they were kicking the man while he was lying in the road.

It was fun, but I didn't think about it much. I wouldn't really say
it made me pray, although it did make me look at the details of
the story quite a lot. I think it might be better with a different
story that I didn't know so well.

I tried it again a bit later with the Christmas story at my youth
group: a friend and I did the birth of Jesus, some other people
did the census, some did the Angel Gabriel coming to Mary, and
another group did the wise men coming to see him. It was really
fun doing it with other people and it was good splitting the story
up into different scenes. Thinking about the story to model it was a
really good way of making me picture the story and having to think
about what it would have looked like, and what was really going on

Other experimenters' notes

8/10 – A really effective way of slowing down and working through a verse or passage. Makes you think about how it would have happened. (Josh, 16)

8.5/10 – I CONSTRUCTED THE SCENE WHERE JESUS VISITED THE DISCIPLES AFTER HIS RESURRECTION. IT WAS REALLY FUN. (FLETCHER, 14)

8 or 9/10 – I did the sea and Jesus story, in Lego, and it did kind of help me connect with God, seeing it visually. (Matthew, 14)

9/10 - I really liked doing this. I did the story of the Good Samaritan, and I made a model of the Samaritan taking the man who was attacked to the inn. I had him on a stretcher as I couldn't find or make a donkey, and then a bed in the inn. I built a desk for the innkeeper and had the Samaritan giving him money to look after the stranger. It really made me think about the story. (Toby, 9)

7/10 - I DID THIS WITH MY YOUTH GROUP, AND WE ALL DID SCENES FROM THE EPIPHANY STORY. IT WAS A NICE WAY OF BRINGING IT ALL TOGETHER AND MAKING IT MORE CREATIVE. MAKING THE STORY WAS MUCH MORE INVOLVING THAN JUST READING IT, IT BROUGHT YOU INTO THE WHOLE EXPERIENCE. AS I WAS BUILDING IT, IT GAVE ME TIME TO REALLY THINK ABOUT THE WHOLE STORY, AND IT MADE ME SEE NEW THINGS ABOUT THE PASSAGE.

IT WAS ALSO REALLY GOOD DOING IT WITH A GROUP. HAVING FRIENDS AROUND ME MADE IT FEEL MORE INCLUSIVE AND A FUN THING TO BE DOING. AND THEN WHEN WE HAD ALL BUILT OUR SCENE WE GOT TO SHOW THEM TO EACH OTHER AND SEE WHAT EVERYONE ELSE HAD DONE. PEOPLE HAD PUT A DIFFERENT SPIN ON THINGS AND IT GAVE ME A DIFFERENT PERSPECTIVE ON THE STORY. (RACHEL, 15)

Pearls
of
Life

Praying with beads

Using beads to help you pray has a long history. The most commonly known version is the rosary, which is especially popular in Roman Catholic devotion as an aid to a set of prayers focusing on Mary, the mother of Jesus. The traditional rosary has five sets of ten small beads, with each set separated by a single larger bead. The Lord's Prayer is said at the beginning of each set, then a short prayer to Mary is said ten times, while at the same time the person praying thinks about a particular prayer topic or 'mystery'. The rosary is a development of much older prayer aids using knotted string or rope, with prayers said as your fingers pass along each knot.

Praying like this is quite different from most modern forms of prayer, which emphasize a personal conversation with God. Instead, these historic forms of prayer focus on simply reciting set prayers a number of times. This idea has sometimes been criticized for being superstitious, and for treating the saying of prayers like a kind of magic spell, but many people find that using a prayer method like this helps them to focus on God.

The idea is usually threefold. Put very simply, it works as follows:

1. Each bead, or knot, reminds you to pray for something.

2. Your hands and mind are kept busy by touching the beads, so you are less likely to be distracted by other things.

3. The physical action of taking up the beads and going through
    them one by one makes you take time out to pray.

The picture above is of a modern example of prayer beads, the 'Pearls
of Life'. These were invented in 1995 by a Swedish bishop named
Martin Lonnebo, who was deliberately trying to come up with a
modern version of prayer beads that helped people to think not just
about Mary, but about their relationship with God. If you want to
read more, he has written a whole book about how he came to
invent them, and how to use them: *Pearls of Life: For the personal
spiritual journey* (Wild Goose Publications, 2007). Although you can
buy the beads ready made to go with the book, if you wish, I think
they are much more personal and meaningful if you make them
yourself – and making them helps you remember the meaning of
each bead, too.

The experiment

THIS EXERCISE INVOLVES FIRST MAKING YOUR OWN
PRAYER BRACELET, AND THEN WEARING IT AND USING IT.

So first, you will need a stock of beads (or buttons would do), and a
piece of string, wool or elastic.

The picture on page 109 shows the original 'Pearls of Life' layout:
you can copy this, or you could make a simpler version of your own.
The suggested sizes and colours given here will help you remember
what each bead represents, but you could choose whatever you like,
or whatever is available easily.

1. Tie a knot in the string first, or the beads will all slip off when
    you put them on! Then choose a large gold bead (or another
    one that seems special to you), and start by putting this on
    the string. This is the God bead.

2. Find six plain beads – in the picture they are long and wooden.
    These are used to create space between the special beads, and
    are called the beads of Silence, or peace. Put one on next, and
    set the others aside to use later on.

3. The third bead represents you! Try to find a
    small pearl-like bead, or another one that you
    feel represents you best.

4. A large white bead comes next: this one represents your baptism, becoming and being a member of the Church.

5. Put another Silence bead on, then a bigger sandy-coloured, maybe rough-textured, bead. This is the Desert bead, and represents the rough and bleak parts of your life.

6. Another Silence bead, then a big blue bead: this is called the Carefree bead. It might remind you of the sky, or the sea. This one represents being happy and relaxed, and trusting God.

7. Add another Silence bead, and then two big red beads. These represent God's love for us in Jesus being born, and in Jesus dying for us – the incarnation and the crucifixion.

8. Then come three small Mystery beads. They might be pearls, or silver, or whatever you like. These are for your most important things or people to pray for and about. You could choose one for each thing or person, or each, one can hold a whole group of concerns. For example, one could stand for your family, one for friends, one for issues that you are worrying about.

9. Next, add a big black bead to represent Night, death and darkness.

10. Then add another Silence bead, and then a final big white bead for Resurrection, before you finish with the last Silence bead.

Make your bracelet following this pattern, and then either wear it
as a constant reminder of prayer, or just pick it up and use it.

There aren't particular set prayers to use, but if you want more
reflection on the different beads you could try googling 'Pearls of
Life', or reading Bishop Lonnebo's book, to find prayers or meditations
written about each bead. But the main way of using the beads is
simply to go through them one by one.

Touch the first bead with your fingers: hold it between finger and
thumb. Think for a bit about what it means to you, today. Then
move on to the next one. Remember what it represents: think about
it for a few seconds, or a few minutes. When you get to a Silence
bead, just sit in silence for a minute or two. And so on, all round the
bracelet.

Feedback

WHEN I TRIED THIS EXPERIMENT, I FOUND . . .

DOING THIS KIND OF PRAYER MADE ME FEEL . . .

THE THING I LIKED BEST ABOUT IT WAS . . .

THINGS I WOULD TRY CHANGING NEXT TIME:

MARKS OUT OF 10:

Noah's review: 8/10

This was quite fun and interactive. Making it didn't really feel like a prayer, though, just a fun craft activity, but the whole experience of making and using it was good.

It was quite easy to remember which bead was which when you were using it, because they were all different – for example, I'd chosen the biggest, shiniest one to represent God.

When it came to praying with it, I went round holding each bead in turn, and then praying about the thing that bead was for.

At the God bead, I found I mainly prayed for the big things, the big topics that I thought God should do something about – world peace, natural disasters, that sort of thing. At the Silence beads, I just sat in silence for a while, but I did find that my mind tended to wander to other things.

I liked the Desert bead, as that was a chance to pray for the rough times in my life, times when I've been bullied or felt a failure. I don't normally think of praying for those things, so it was good to have the bead to tell me to pray for them.

At the second red one I prayed – you know how Jesus died to save us from our sins? Well, I prayed that that contract hadn't run out, so to speak, and that that still was the case for everyone nowadays.

I decided that for me, the first Mystery bead was for my friends and family, the second one was for places experiencing bad things and conflicts, and the third one represented nature and the environment. They stayed the same each time.

I usually found I spent about the same amount of time on each bead, except I spent more time on one of the Mystery beads, which I'd decided was representing places in particular conflict and need.

Overall, I liked using the beads. It was really interactive because I'd made it myself, I was wearing it, and I could use it whenever I wanted. It was really good that it was something you could wear in public without looking stupid. Because the God bead was the biggest, I had to wear it with that on top of my wrist (or it was uncomfortable when I put my hand down) and I found that every time I glanced down and saw it, it reminded me of God.

Other experimenters' notes

8/10 – I found that the bead ideas really meant something to me. It was really relaxing to do, and made me think about all the different things that the beads represented. I think it will help me to remember to pray. I find I do have to use my hands to do things, so touching the beads will really help. (Evelyn, 15)

9/10 – I REALLY ENJOYED DOING THIS: THE WHOLE EXPERIENCE OF MAKING IT, AND USING IT AFTERWARDS. I REALLY LIKED THE SYMBOLISM, AND THAT IT WAS QUITE UNDERSTATED – NOBODY ELSE LOOKING AT IT WOULD UNDERSTAND IT.

I DIDN'T HAVE BEADS SO I USED BUTTONS. WHILE I WAS MAKING IT, I WASN'T PRAYING AS SUCH, BUT THE FEELING OF BEING SURROUNDED BY THE SPIRIT WAS QUITE OVERWHELMING; IT WAS REALLY SPECIAL.

I KEPT THE BEADS AT THE END OF MY BED AND USED THEM TO PRAY WITH. IT TOOK ME A COUPLE OF DAYS TO REMEMBER WHAT THEY ALL MEANT, SO TO BEGIN WITH I HAD TO KEEP THE INSTRUCTIONS BY MY BED AND REFER TO THEM. THEN IN THE MORNING I WOULD SEE IT THERE ON MY BED AND BE REMINDED OF ALL THE THINGS. IT WAS CONSTANTLY ON MY MIND AS I WAS IN MY ROOM. (RACHEL, 15)

Labyrinth

What's a labyrinth?

A labyrinth looks like a flat maze, with a way in and out and a path to the centre. But a labyrinth differs from a maze, because it only has one path. The path winds round and back on itself, so you can seem suddenly very near the centre, then very far away. There are various different designs, some more complex than others, but whichever one you are using you know you can't get lost. All you have to do to get to the centre is simply keep following the path.

Labyrinths are normally circular, and can be very big – as much as 15 metres in diameter. Full-size labyrinths like this are sometimes set in stone into church floors (famously at Chartres Cathedral in France), and are sometimes laid out in gardens in turf or as brick paths. Smaller versions can be drawn on a handkerchief and kept in your pocket, or printed on paper or a tile, or carved into wood.

Labyrinths have been used since ancient times as symbols of the spiritual life, and since at least medieval times as symbols of the Christian path. They were used as an alternative to costly and impractical pilgrimages for people who couldn't easily travel. The journey to the middle of the labyrinth might represent travelling to Jerusalem, or meeting God face to face, or reaching the end of life.

Using labyrinths

There are various ways to use a labyrinth, but the pure method, with a full-size labyrinth, is simply to slowly follow the path to the centre, rest there a while, and then slowly follow it back out. It is a method of praying using your whole body. You don't just sit there and think, your body actually makes a journey. In my experience of walking full-size labyrinths, I have found that my mind follows that physical journey, and is able to make some connections that I'm not sure I'd have made if I were just sitting still. An alternative is to use the labyrinth to think about a particular question, or to reflect on a particular issue, as you walk. Some people read a scriptural quotation on the way in, and perhaps another on the way out. Some might deliberately think about their own journey through life as they walk.

The experiment

FIRST, FIND YOUR LABYRINTH. FULL-SIZE
LABYRINTHS ARE BIG, EXPENSIVE AND TIME-
CONSUMING TO BUILD, BUT IF THERE IS ONE
NEAR YOU THEN DO GIVE WALKING IT A TRY.
I HAVE AN OAK FINGER LABYRINTH, ABOUT 18 INCHES ACROSS,
WITH A GROOVED PATH CARVED INTO THE WOOD; YOU MIGHT BE
ABLE TO FIND ONE OF THESE TO BORROW LOCALLY. MOST EASILY,
YOU CAN PRINT OUT A SIMPLE LABYRINTH PATTERN FROM THE
INTERNET (JUST GOOGLE 'LABYRINTH PATTERN').

Once you have your labyrinth, it is time to 'walk' it. Simply trace the
path, either with your finger or with a pen. Try to go quite slowly.
Notice how you feel. Do you feel you want to go faster? Do you
find any parts of the path more frustrating, or annoying, or fun than
others? When you get to the middle, stop for a while. How does it
feel to be there? How do you feel about following the path back
out again? When you feel ready, follow the path out, again noticing
how you feel.

One youth group that did this experiment laminated the print-outs
and used marker pens to trace the paths: if you do this, you could
use a different colour for going in and going out. You could also
trace the pattern onto cloth and use fabric pens to make it
permanent. You can either just follow the path and see where your
thoughts take you, or you might prefer to use some words to focus
on. Why not try doing the labyrinth twice, and give both a try?

When you use words, I suggest the first time thinking about two things that Jesus said about being a path for us to follow. You could think about Jesus saying 'I am the way, the truth and the life' on the way in; and on the way out, think about the words 'Follow me'. Or, if there is a particular question that is bothering you, try asking God to help you think about that as you follow the path, and see what happens.

Feedback

WHEN I TRIED THIS EXPERIMENT, I FOUND . . .

WALKING THE LABYRINTH MADE ME FEEL . . .

THE THING I LIKED BEST ABOUT IT WAS . . .

THINGS I WOULD TRY CHANGING NEXT TIME:

MARKS OUT OF 10:

Noah's review:

7/10 with the set words: made me pray but more limiting

8/10 just going round: this really made me think

I used a wooden labyrinth that I could hold in my hands. I started by following the labyrinth with my finger, and thinking about the words suggested. To begin with, I was just saying the words to myself, and I didn't really know what to do, quite frankly. So then I started thinking about the words — and saying 'if you are the way or the light or whatever, show me' — and I suppose I was thinking about what it meant for God to be the way, etc., and asking him to help me understand that. After I'd done that, I tried using a marble to go round the engraved track. This was much more fun, and I had to really concentrate on communicating with my body.

I actually did it twice with the marble, because the first time I just concentrated on getting the marble round the track, and realized at the end I didn't get it as a prayer at all. So I did it again, and the second time I was more just letting it go round and not trying so hard to follow the path exactly, and letting the marble jump corners and walls. I didn't think much on the way in, but on the way out that time I found myself thinking about how it compares to life.

I mean, when you were rolling the marble around and trying to get it right, it kept jumping corners and going over the lines, but you got there in the end. I thought this was sort of like the journey of life: you try to get somewhere and when it feels that you're really, really close, you get turned away by little things, and then they turn into bigger things, and then you sort them out and they seem to be coming back into the perfect life and you are coming back into the centre again. And then more little things go wrong, more arguments with friends and family or whatever happen again, so you sometimes feel like you're not getting anywhere. But then things start to get better again.

Summing up the whole experience I would definitely recommend using the labyrinth, but I wouldn't use set words again.

Other experimenters' notes

8/10 – I was able to sit and think clearly about things that were on my mind. Doing this kind of prayer made me feel calm and clear-headed. I could sit and think about things and be relaxed by the labyrinth taking my mind off other things. I used a paper print-out of a Celtic style labyrinth, and I'd like to try again with a longer labyrinth. (Luke, 16)

9/10 – USING THE LABYRINTH WAS VERY CALM AND RELAXING. ALSO, WHEN I WAS THINKING ABOUT THE PHRASES IT REALLY MADE ME THINK OF THEM IN A DIFFERENT WAY. I'D DO IT AGAIN USING DIFFERENT PHRASES TO THINK ABOUT. (RACHEL, 15)

7/10 – When I tried this, I found that it was quite a simple task, so this allowed me to think while going round the labyrinth. Doing it made me feel very calm, and made me really think about stuff. The only thing I might change for next time would be to use a slightly more colourful labyrinth than the plain wooden one I was using: but nothing too dramatic. (Chris, 15)

8/10 - Following the labyrinth made you think about your spiritual journey. It made me feel that God was always with me as I was on his path, and it really gave you time to connect with God. If possible, I'd like to try walking a full-size labyrinth myself now. (Jonny, 14)

8/10

- I REALLY ENJOYED TRACING MY FINGER AROUND THE LABYRINTH AS IT FOCUSED ME IN AND MADE ME THINK OF ONE OF THE ISSUES I AM STRUGGLING WITH. WHEN I WAS 'WALKING' THROUGH THE LABYRINTH, I FELT I WASN'T ALONE BUT WAS WALKING WITH JESUS. I WAS REMINDED OF THE IDEA OF GOD ALWAYS BEING WITH US AND WALKING ALONGSIDE US.
- I USED A PAPER LABYRINTH, AND WHEN CERTAIN WORDS OR PRAYERS CAME TO ME, I WROTE THEM DOWN ON THE PATH.
- A FEW OF US USED PENS TO TRACE OUR JOURNEY. CHANGING COLOUR ON THE WAY OUT WAS A GOOD WAY OF HELPING US TO THINK OF THIS AS A TWO-WAY JOURNEY – ONE TO A PLACE WHERE WE TOOK OUR PRAYER TO GOD AND ANOTHER WHERE WE THEN BEGAN TO WALK BACK INTO THE WORLD SLOWLY COMING OUT OF PRAYER.

(MEMBERS OF 3GENERATE)

Breathing meditation

What is meditation?

Meditation is a kind of prayer that involves setting time aside to be calm and at peace. It is very different from most other types of prayer in that it is not about talking to God, or even listening to God, but just being. The aim is simply to sit there, trying to free your mind from thinking about anything in particular. You are not trying to achieve anything, or say anything, or do anything: you are just taking time to be. Meditation is an important part of many spiritual traditions. In our modern society it is most often associated with Buddhism, but it is also a very ancient Christian practice.

In the Christian tradition, meditation tends to be called contemplative prayer. In Christian contemplation, the underlying assumption is that when you spend time just being, you are being with God. You don't even have to busy yourself thinking good thoughts about God: just be, and let yourself become aware of yourself in God's presence.

Meditative techniques

When you try it, you may well find that it is surprisingly hard to simply sit still in silence, even for a few minutes. Because people tend to find this very difficult, various different practices have developed to help you focus. The two main ones are concentrating on your breathing, and repeating the same word or phrase over and over – usually either in silence, or just under your breath. These are well-known techniques in virtually every spiritual tradition. They are often combined, so that you say a word, or part of a phrase, as you breathe in, and repeat it, or say the other part of the phrase, as you breathe out.

The actual word or phrase (known as a 'mantra' in some spiritual traditions) isn't important. It is simply there to help you meditate, rather than saying it being the point of the exercise (and it certainly doesn't have any sort of magical power). The phrase most commonly used in the Christian tradition is a very old, short prayer known as the Jesus Prayer: 'Jesus Christ, Son of God, have mercy on me, a sinner'. Other people use a favourite Bible verse, or simply the word 'God' or 'Jesus'. Don't worry about choosing the 'right' word. For now, I suggest that you use the Jesus Prayer if you want to use words.

Some people also find visualization helpful. You can begin your meditation by imagining going into a secluded, beautiful place – somewhere you are alone and safe, and can leave whenever you want. Imagine yourself walking across a threshold into that place: going through a gateway or door, or down some steps, and then sitting there. For example, you could imagine walking down some steps into a sunken garden, or through a gate into a meadow, or along a path through sand dunes to a beach.

How it works

Physically, concentrating on your breathing calms you down and makes you more aware of your own body. Mentally, it helps you to free your mind from distractions, and it gives you something to focus on while you deliberately choose to take time out of your busy life to spend that time on prayer or meditation.

Spiritually, doing this helps us to focus on who we really are in relation to God. All the things that we do and say to try to give a good impression to other people are stripped away. It also gives us space to listen to God: but don't let 'trying to hear God' become the point of the exercise! The aim is simply to be: don't expect any particular results.

The experiment

YOU ARE GOING TO TRY MEDITATING, JUST FOR A SHORT PERIOD.

First, find somewhere you can be comfortable, still and undisturbed. Most people sit, but find the position that is most comfortable for you.

Now set an alarm on your phone, etc., for the amount of time you are going to set aside. I suggest that you start with 10 minutes – you may want to build up to 20 minutes or half an hour over time.

Then shut your eyes, and begin to concentrate on your breathing. Be aware of each breath in . . . and out. If you are saying the Jesus Prayer, say a phrase on each breath, in and out. You will probably find that your breathing begins to slow down.

After a while, become conscious of your body: of the weight of your limbs, how it feels to be sitting. You might find that you begin to feel uncomfortable or self-conscious. You might also find yourself disturbed by noises from outside your room. Just notice what you are feeling or hearing. Notice it kindly, don't tell yourself off for being distracted by it. Mentally acknowledge what is there, then focus on your breathing again.

It is completely normal to find that all sorts of thoughts and worries come rushing in – from big important things that you must remember to do, to all sorts of trivialities. It is also normal to find

131

suddenly that your mind is wandering. Again, don't worry. When you notice a thought, a worry or a feeling, or realize that your mind has wandered, just notice it kindly, and then consciously return your focus to your breathing. It is when you are distracted like this that repeating something like the Jesus Prayer can be particularly helpful, as it gives you something to focus on.

Doing this may well feel really weird. We are very rarely still and silent, with nothing to keep our minds occupied. So when we do find ourselves in such a situation, it can feel very uncomfortable. Even those who make a habit of doing this for half an hour or more a day find it difficult at times. You may find yourself getting very annoyed. Just accept any weirdness and discomfort, notice it, and keep concentrating on your breathing.

If you are using the Jesus Prayer, you may want to drop parts of it as you go, so that it gets shorter. In the end, you may be left with only one or two words, just repeating those on the in and out breaths.

Keep at it until your alarm sounds. If you visualized going somewhere, now visualize leaving that place: walking back out across the threshold, knowing you can return whenever you want. If you were using the Jesus Prayer, say it one last time and then say 'Amen', out loud.

Feedback

WHEN I TRIED THIS EXPERIMENT, I FOUND . . .

DOING THIS KIND OF PRAYER MADE ME FEEL . . .

THE THING I LIKED BEST ABOUT IT WAS . . .

THINGS I WOULD TRY CHANGING NEXT TIME:

MARKS OUT OF 10:

Noah's review: 9/10

This was definitely not as easy as some of the other experiments but it was a very nice experience.

I did get distracted and kept finding myself being sidetracked. For the first few minutes, I was just sitting there concentrating on my breathing. That was probably the most relaxing bit. Then coming out of that I started thinking about God, because thinking about breathing made me think about God designing us and making us, and how complicated a process even breathing is. Then I found myself thinking about other stuff — like school and so on — and then when I realized that I'd got distracted I started using the Jesus Prayer. That was very helpful, because saying the prayer did help me come back to focusing on the breathing. Then for a while I started actually praying even though I wasn't meant to, but all through I was concentrating on inhaling and exhaling, and that started affecting what I was praying for. So I prayed for all the usual stuff like friends, family and conflicts, and then I prayed for people who sometimes find it hard to breathe, who have lung diseases and so on, and that led me on to praying for sick people in general.

I didn't have an alarm handy, so I stopped when I thought I'd done ten minutes but I think it was more like seven or eight minutes actually!

I will probably do this again, because at the end of the time I felt so peaceful and refreshed, like I'd just woken up from a really good sleep. After I got up I felt really relaxed and invigorated.

Other experimenters' notes

9/10 - I thought this was really good, especially for someone who has anxiety like me as it did help calm me. I really liked this, though I wasn't expecting to. When I first read it I thought it was a load of rubbish, but actually it was the most spiritual of the ones I've tried, and really relaxing.

I just concentrated on my breathing at first, and that helped relax me. I could feel my pulse go down. Then after a while I tried singing the Jesus Prayer - sort of chanting it. That felt really spiritual and relaxing, because you just had one thing to focus on and there was nothing else.

I did have quite a lot of distractions though! Notifications kept going off on my phone with a little pinging sound and I kept checking them. So I'd suggest turning off the internet or your phone would be good when you try this.

I thought setting the timer was good, because I didn't have to worry about how long I'd done it for and I could check how much I'd done. I'd do it for longer next time though - maybe I'll try to do a minute more each time. (Jasmine, 14)

4/10 – I SET A TIMER ON MY PHONE AND CLOSED MY EYES AND LISTENED TO MY BREATHING PATTERN. WHEN I TRIED THIS EXPERIMENT I FOUND THAT IT DIDN'T HELP ME TO THINK ABOUT GOD AND JESUS MORE AND I COULDN'T REALLY THINK ABOUT ANYTHING OTHER THAN MY BREATHING. DOING THIS KIND OF PRAYER MADE ME FEEL EXHAUSTED BECAUSE WHENEVER I SHUT MY EYES I JUST FEEL TIRED. THE BEST THING ABOUT IT WAS THAT MY BRAIN GOT TO UNWIND AND SHUT DOWN FOR A LITTLE BIT. SOMETHING THAT I WOULD TRY CHANGING NEXT TIME ABOUT THE EXPERIMENT WOULD BE THE AMOUNT OF TIME THAT I HAD TO SHUT MY EYES FOR. MAYBE I'D ONLY SHUT THEM FOR A COUPLE OF MINUTES TO TRY AND PRAY, BECAUSE I JUST THINK THAT TEN MINUTES IS TOO LONG. (BEATRICE, 15)

8/10 – I found it quite easy to meditate, but I found sitting still made me light-headed after a few minutes. I sat with my back to the TV and concentrated on breathing in and out. With absolutely no distractions I was fine with sitting still, but as I said I got a bit light-headed from sitting upright.

It's a really good technique for calming down after a stressful day and it really helps. (Hannah, 10)

6/10 - I think that this method is effective at assisting prayer, as long as you can keep yourself from getting distracted. This is not easy, even if you notice in time to return to your original thoughts. Some people may struggle to sit still and stay inactive for long, so I would suggest using music to give an external locus of thought.

Personally, I didn't think too much about God while doing this because I was concentrating on breathing. Overall, I would recommend this to other people as it would most likely make prayer easier. (Callum, 15)

7/10 – I WENT INTO MY ROOM, CLOSED THE CURTAINS AND SWITCHED THE LIGHTS OFF. THEN I LAY ON MY BED WITH MY EYES CLOSED, SET THE TIMER, AND REPEATED THE JESUS PRAYER FOR TEN MINUTES. IT REALLY MADE ME FEEL CONCENTRATED, AND CLOSER TO GOD. IT MADE ME FEEL LIKE I COULD JUST BE ON MY OWN WITH GOD, THERE WAS NOTHING TO DISTRACT ME. THINGS CAME INTO MY HEAD A BIT, BUT THEN I JUST SAID THAT WAS SOMETHING I'M THANKFUL FOR, OR WHATEVER, AND CARRIED ON REPEATING THE WORDS. HAVING THE WORDS TO SAY MEANT I KNEW EXACTLY WHAT I WAS DOING. (REUBEN, 13)

Nerf gun confession

Missing the mark

One of the words in the Bible that is normally translated as 'sinning' literally means something more like 'missing the mark'. It is a term from archery, about aiming for the target – aiming for a bullseye, perfection – but more often than not, falling short or going wildly off course.

Target practice can help us to think about what this really means, and how it feels to miss the mark. We want to hit it; we are aiming at it; but when we are a long way from the target, to our frustration, we find it very difficult to get that elusive bullseye.

Christian tradition tells us that we are so far from God that it is inevitable that we will miss the mark most of the time. But the good news is that God isn't keeping score. God is happy so long as we are trying to aim in the right direction.

If you try target shooting but are facing away from the target, it won't matter how good a shot you are. You are only going to get further away from the target if you shoot further. Just as in target shooting, in living as a Christian the most important thing to get right first is to be facing in the right direction.

That's why, in the baptism service, when someone becomes a Christian, he or she is asked a series of questions about turning from all that denies God, and turning to God. In many churches, people will actually be asked to turn around at that point, as a sign of their commitment to going through life facing in the right direction. What matters in being a Christian is not how far on you are, but what direction you are facing in.

Practising to improve

In most Christian churches, a confession happens in the main weekly church service, and Christians often also confess to God as part of their own regular private prayers. By confessing – naming where we have missed the mark – we are acknowledging that we have missed the target of living like Jesus (which of course we will!), we remind ourselves to make sure we are still facing in the right direction, and we commit ourselves to not give up bothering to hit the target, but to keep practising.

And just as with target shooting, we will get better with practice. Missing the mark in target practice isn't failure. In fact, if you are seriously trying to improve your shooting, then when you have got so good that you are hitting the target every time from a particular distance you will move further back to give yourself a new challenge. When you are trying to improve at any sport, you keep pushing yourself. Missing the mark if you are practising hard enough is an inevitable and good part of learning.

The very best target shooters practise loads. And someone who becomes an Olympic gold medallist at shooting doesn't stop practising just because they have got good enough – if they did, they would quickly lose their touch. Similarly, confession is something we keep doing as Christians, and even the most experienced Christians, even the holiest saints, keep doing it. In fact, just like with sports, the people who are the very best are the ones who practise most! Maybe that's what we mean when we call someone a 'practising Christian'?

The experiment

SO HAVE A GO AT SOME TARGET SHOOTING NOW. CHOOSE A
TARGET, AND GRAB YOUR GUN OR BOW – SOMETHING LIKE
A NERF GUN THAT SHOOTS FOAM DARTS IS IDEAL.

First try shooting in the wrong direction. Stand in front of the
target, but then deliberately turn away from it and shoot. How
does that feel?

Then turn back to face the target, and try shooting from one metre
away. It should be quite easy to hit the target from here. Now try
moving back, and shooting from further and further away until you
are mainly missing the target (how far you have to go will depend
on how good a shot you are!).

Each time you hit the target, think of one thing you did today or
this week that was right on the mark, and thank God for that.

Each time you miss, think of one thing you did today or this week
that missed the mark – a word that hurt someone, an opportunity for
kindness missed, being in a rush so that you didn't give someone your
full attention, or maybe deliberate rudeness or wrongdoing. Admit
that was a missing of the mark, and then try shooting again.

Feedback

WHEN I TRIED THIS EXPERIMENT, I FOUND . . .

DOING THIS KIND OF PRAYER MADE ME FEEL . . .

THE THING I LIKED BEST ABOUT IT WAS . . .

THINGS I WOULD TRY CHANGING NEXT TIME:

MARKS OUT OF 10:

Noah's review: 7.5/10

The idea of praying with a weapon is quite strange, but it's quite appealing too! It felt an odd thing to do at first, but I actually really enjoyed it.

Starting off facing in the wrong direction felt really weird. I wasn't shooting the right way at all and didn't have any chance of hitting the target! Turning round felt good. It did make me think a bit about the idea of conversion, there was a real sense of relief to have turned round.

Then I got on with shooting. I used a tree in my back garden as the target, and I'm quite good at shooting Nerf guns, so I totally destroyed that tree!

Personally, since in the last few months I've been having quite a rough time, this really worked very well for me. The idea of hitting the mark and missing the mark made a lot of sense to me. And actually doing the shooting, not just reading about the idea, really helped bring it to life and made it seem much more real.

The idea of praying for things that had gone well when I hit and for things that had gone badly when I missed worked really well too. In fact, I think this was one of the best ideas.

Other experimenters' notes

9/10 – This was really good for reflecting on what you've done good and bad in your own life. I found it made me really focus on specific things I'd done, and where I'd gone wrong, and it made me think about how I could try to put that right. (Dan, 16)

4/10 – I THOUGHT THIS WAS A HORRENDOUS METAPHOR! WE TRIED DOING THIS AS A YOUTH GROUP BUT WE DIDN'T CONCENTRATE ON SHOOTING AT THE TARGET FOR VERY LONG, IT JUST DESCENDED INTO A NERF WAR VERY QUICKLY. IN A WAY THAT WAS QUITE FRIGHTENING: WE WERE TRYING TO BE HOLY AND WE JUST STARTED SHOOTING EACH OTHER. IT MADE ME THINK ABOUT ALL THE WARS THERE ARE ALL AROUND THE WORLD AND HOW AGGRESSIVE PEOPLE CAN BE, SO I SUPPOSE IT DID MAKE ME THINK, BUT I DIDN'T FEEL COMFORTABLE DOING THIS AT ALL. (LUKE, 17)

6.5/10 – I thought this was really fun, and it was a good concept. But although I thought it was a clever way of thinking about it, I found it didn't really help me focus on prayer.

Starting off shooting by facing in the wrong direction felt really annoying, when I could have just turned round and hit the target. I suppose that was the point, for it to feel frustrating? But then when I did turn round, I realized afterwards that I had spent most of the time focusing on trying to hit the target rather than thinking about the concept! It became quite frustrating because I was quite a bad shot. (Jasmine, 14)

9/10 - I taped a piece of paper to the wall with a target on, then stood a metre away and shot in the other direction. Then I turned round and shot at the target - and got a bullseye! Then I shot at it again from five metres away and ten metres away - then there was a wall so I couldn't go any further.

After that, I sat down for a few minutes to think about hitting and missing my goals in life. I thought about how sometimes I can be rather astray, like the bullet went astray. The idea of sin as missing the mark isn't often conveyed in that way, normally sin just means doing something bad, so it was an interesting way of thinking about it. (Reuben, 13)

Examen

Praying through your day

Do you sometimes feel stuck for what to pray about? Sometimes we can get in a rut or feel that there is nothing particular to pray about today. One way of avoiding this is to use the Christian tradition of the 'Examen'. This is a structured way of reflecting through prayer on the past 24 hours, which means you never have to worry about finding something to pray for or about! Everyone always has the past day to reflect on.

The idea is to walk through your day in your memory, noticing times when you felt any particularly strong emotions or feelings – whether positive or negative – and any incidents or encounters that seem to stick in your mind, or to leap out at you as you think back. The things that jump out at you, or that are associated with strong emotions, are things that it is worth thinking about more closely.

Why do this?

Spending some time at the end of the day examining what has gone on is an old Christian tradition, particularly associated with St Ignatius. It was advocated by some Greek philosophers before Christianity too. Often called the 'Examination of Conscience', it is the traditional way in which Roman Catholics were taught to prepare for confession to a priest: go through everything you can remember doing, and examine carefully what your motivations were. In the past, the emphasis was very much on looking for sins,

148

but the modern approach to the Examen is to focus on closely examining your consciousness, and especially your feelings and emotions.

The idea is that God is found in our everyday lives. By paying attention in prayer to the detail of our day-to-day activities – the trip to school, an argument on the bus, a person you met, a moment when you felt surprising anger, joy, fear or excitement – the Examen helps us to get used to seeing all of life as a place where God meets with us. The incarnation – God being born as a human at Christmas – is a sign of this. So too are the sacraments of the Church, like Holy Communion or Baptism: moments when God is encountered in normal things, like bread, wine and water.

The Examen also helps you to take your own emotions and feelings seriously. Reflecting on them helps to develop a reflective wisdom about yourself. If you make a habit of it, you will find that you gradually become less swept away by strong feelings, but develop the wisdom to examine them, see what is really going on there, and come to understand what your emotions are signalling to you.

The experiment

THERE ARE SIX STEPS TO THE EXAMEN.

1. Start with a short prayer for understanding or light. Pray that God will shine a torch on the things you should be concentrating on as you go through the day.

2. Then begin by looking for good things, things to be thankful for. Go back over the past 24 hours noticing things that were good, enjoyable, or seemed especially meaningful. It could be anything: a flower in the wall that you noticed on the way to school, a conversation that struck you, time with a friend. Say thank you to God for the things that occur to you.

3. Now imagine yourself walking back through the day. Follow yourself in your imagination: where did you go, who did you see? Notice the feelings that rise up as you remember the day, positive and negative, and notice too any incidents that jump out at you.

4. Choose one of these things to focus on, the one that is associated with the strongest feelings. It doesn't matter if the feeling is positive or negative (that will vary from day to day). Trust that the thing that jumps out at you is the one God wants you to examine more closely, even if it seems trivial or painful. The fact that it jumps out at you is the result of the prayer for enlightenment that you began with.

Now imagine picking up that incident, and turning it around in the air, looking carefully at it – like a jeweller examining all the different facets of a diamond. Think about what was really going on. What led up to it? Why did you react the way you did? What were your real motivations for what you did, or said? How does looking at it now make you feel?

Ask God if there is anything else you should notice about it. Pray for anything that has arisen out of your examination.

Then, if there were two or three things that jumped out at you as you reviewed the day, you might want to do this again for each of them.

5. Next, think briefly about the day to come. Mentally walk through what you are expecting to happen: your timetable, any encounters or activities you are looking forward to or are concerned about. Again, note what your feelings or emotions are as you imagine going through tomorrow. Pray about anything that arises.

6. Finally, imagine handing over to God all the things you have thought about. You could imagine literally picking them all up and putting them at the foot of the cross: things you are grateful for, things you are worried about, whatever your thoughts have led you to. End by saying the Lord's Prayer.

Feedback

WHEN I TRIED THIS EXPERIMENT, I FOUND . . .

DOING THIS KIND OF PRAYER MADE ME FEEL . . .

THE THING I LIKED BEST ABOUT IT WAS . . .

THINGS I WOULD TRY CHANGING NEXT TIME:

MARKS OUT OF 10:

152

Noah's review: 8/10

I found it quite hard to do the thankfulness bit, because although I'd had fun today I kept thinking that I hadn't really done anything to help other people. I was thankful for the opportunity God had given me to have fun with my friends and family, but I felt a bit guilty that there had probably been lots of opportunities to help people that I'd missed.

At first I couldn't really think of any strong emotions, but when I thought about it more I realized you do feel quite a lot of strong emotions every day. So today I realized I was playing board games earlier, and when I was winning I felt very happy and rejoicing, but when I was losing I felt annoyed or even enraged.

It was easy to identify a particular incident to think about, and I found examining that was fun and interesting. The specific questions helped me to think about it.

The part I found most engaging was praying for tomorrow. You sometimes forget to pray for yourself and just pray for others and the world: praying that what I was going to do tomorrow would be important or useful was not just praying for myself but also for others, so it combined the two.

Ending with the Lord's Prayer was quite nice, because when I was a little kid my parents always used to sing it to me when they put me to bed, and so using it was nostalgic and made me think of that sense of safety and comfort.

Other experimenters' notes

8/10 – Thumbs up for this one! I liked the explanation, it was really clear and detailed.

I also found that this was really easy to do. I thought starting with a short prayer was good because that got me into a prayerful mood, and then going over the day in my head helped me focus. I really liked the idea of walking yourself through the day, that really helped me imagine and think of things that I wouldn't have noticed otherwise.

It was good that the feeling you focused on could be either positive or negative, that made it seem much more realistic and recognized that you don't always have good days. And I liked the idea of imagining turning the incident around: it made it easier to visualize or picture the idea, and focus in on it.

I thought thinking about the day ahead was good too, and it made me think about how the future and the past go together and are both important – I got quite philosophical! (Jasmine, 14)

7/10 – I FOUND THAT I STUDIED A POINT IN MY DAY AND THEN ANALYSED WHY I ACTED THAT WAY. I COULD THEN GO ON TO PRAY ABOUT THAT ASPECT OF MY LIFE. OVERALL, I FOUND IT AN EFFECTIVE WAY OF 'UNCLUTTERING' PRAYERS. HOWEVER, IT IS EASY TO GET DISTRACTED BY ONE PART OF YOUR DAY, AND START PLANNING WHAT YOU WILL DO TOMORROW, ETC. (CALLUM, 15)

5/10 – I thought this was good, but I wouldn't do it again for two simple reasons – I would forget and I prefer to pray about things when they happen. I liked the thinking about tomorrow bit. (Hazel, 13)

8/10 – It was nice to sit down and think about the day before, and what you did. It was quite good and relaxing.

In the thanks section I was quite thankful: it did work! Then I think looking back through the day for strong emotions was a really good idea. It was a good thing to sit and do because you just reflect, and you think about how you could have made the day go better.

Thinking about the day to come, we were about to go on holiday so I was thinking about what the journey would be like, and what the weather would be like. I prayed that the weather would be good, and also we were visiting my great-grandma, so I prayed that she was OK.

It was really good how it worked, basically looking over the day and thinking about everything that happened. (Daisy, 13)

Taste
and see

'Taste and see'

'O taste and see that the Lord is good!' exclaims the writer of Psalm
34. And in quite a few places in the Bible, praying, or reading or
hearing the Scriptures, is imagined as being like eating something
sweet and lovely.

Eating as a ritual

When we eat, there are lots of things going on. First, there is taste –
things we like or dislike, things that are sweet or sour or bitter.
Second, there is hunger and nutrition: the food we eat nourishes
our bodies and becomes part of us. Third, when we eat with other
people that experience helps create a community – whether that's
a family Christmas lunch, who you choose to sit with for lunch
at school, or having the neighbours round for a barbecue.

All around the world, people have rituals and celebrations which
involve eating special foods, from the Thanksgiving turkey to the
Spanish tradition of eating 'The Twelve Grapes of Luck' as the clocks
strike twelve on New Year's Eve. Sometimes this involves a sequence
of particular symbolic foodstuffs to remind the community of
important events in the past, as in the Jewish tradition of the
Seder meal, which commemorates the beginning of the feast of
Passover and involves in the retelling of the story in the book of
Exodus, of God leading the ancient Israelites out of slavery in Egypt.

Holy Communion

In the Christian tradition, eating the bread and drinking the wine of Holy Communion is the central religious observance. Communion (which has different names in different traditions – you may know it as Mass, or the Lord's Supper, or the Eucharist) does all sorts of different things. The bread and wine, and the words used in the eucharistic prayer, remind us of Jesus' last supper with his disciples, and remind us that Jesus died for us. Eating and drinking from the same plate and cup binds us together symbolically – and this is reinforced by the words we often say together, 'though we are many, we are one body, because we all share in one bread'. And eating real food which symbolizes and becomes Jesus for us, means that we are choosing to invite God into our lives not just in a vague spiritual sense, but literally into our bodies. By eating something that represents God for us, we can become aware in a very literal way of God becoming an inseparable part of us.

You may already be used to taking communion at your church, or you may be thinking about preparing for it. In this experiment we're not going to attempt to recreate that, because communion isn't a private thing but is something that should be done by the whole church community gathering together. But here, we're going to try experimenting with eating and drinking different symbolic foods to help you reflect on what they represent, and on the act of eating and drinking as a type of prayer.

The experiment

THIS IS ONE OF THE FEW EXPERIMENTS THAT MAY WORK BETTER AS A GROUP ACTIVITY, BECAUSE IT INVOLVES A CERTAIN AMOUNT OF SHOPPING AND PREPARATION, NOT TO MENTION WASHING UP! BUT DON'T BE PUT OFF TRYING THIS IF YOU WOULD PREFER TO DO IT ON YOUR OWN.

First, you will need to get your ingredients together. You will need at least four or five of the foods listed below. Don't worry if you can't get them all, just use what you can most easily find. I would recommend that you do include the first and the last ones on the list, though.

Arrange the foods in a line on a table. Now eat each one slowly, really concentrating on the taste. As you eat it, read the Bible verse or short note that goes with each one. When you have swallowed, while the taste is still in your mouth, say a short prayer in your head asking God to help you really take in that idea.

1 Honey/sugar

> How sweet are your words to my taste,
> sweeter than honey to my mouth!
> (Psalm 119.103)

Pray for enjoyment in reading the Bible and for wisdom in finding pleasure in good things.

2 Apple/pear/banana/peach

In the story of the beginning of the world in Genesis, the writer imagines a garden full of fruit trees, all of which people can eat from except one. But of course, the first people are tempted to eat the fruit of the one tree they have been told not to touch:

> 'You may freely eat of every tree of the garden; but of the tree of the knowledge of good and evil you shall not eat' . . . it was a delight to the eyes, and . . . to be desired to make one wise . . .
>
> (From Genesis 2.16–17; 3.6. Read the whole story in Genesis 2.4—3.24)

Pray for wisdom in knowing good from evil, and for forgiveness when we ignore God.

3 Cucumber/melon

After the people of Israel had been rescued by Moses from slavery in Egypt, and God had fed them miraculously with manna in the desert, they started complaining about being in the desert, and having only manna to eat, and remembering only the good things about their old life:

> The Israelites . . . wept again, and said, 'If only we had meat to eat! We remember the fish we used to eat in Egypt for nothing, the cucumbers, the melons, the leeks, the onions, and the garlic.'
>
> (Numbers 11.4–5; to read the story of the Exodus from Egypt, see Exodus chapters 1—14)

Pray that you may be thankful for what you have, rather than complaining about what you don't have. Pray for wisdom to let the past go, and not worry about what might have been.

4 A glass of water

Most of the Bible stories come from a desert context, where finding a spring of water can literally mean the difference between life and death. One day when Jesus was thirsty, he asked a foreign woman to get him a drink from a well:

> Jesus said to her, 'Everyone who drinks this water will be thirsty again, but those who drink of the water that I will give them will never be thirsty. The water that I will give will become in them a spring of water gushing up to eternal life.'
>
> (John 4.13–14. Read the whole story in John 4.1–42)

Pray for those who don't have clean water to drink, and thank God for our good fortune in having water on tap. Think about what it might mean to never be thirsty for God.

5 A tuna sandwich (or other bread and fish)

Jesus' miraculous feeding of several thousand people with a small amount of bread and fish is the only miracle (apart from his resurrection) which is recorded in all four Gospels – Matthew, Mark, Luke and John.

When it was evening, the disciples came to Jesus and said, 'This is a deserted place, and the hour is now late; send the crowds away so that they may go into the villages and buy food for themselves . . . we have nothing here but five loaves and two fish.' And he said, 'Bring them here to me.' Then he ordered the crowds to sit down on the grass. Taking the five loaves and the two fish, he looked up to heaven, and blessed and broke the loaves, and gave them to the disciples, and the disciples gave them to the crowds. And all ate and were filled; and they took up what was left over of the broken pieces, twelve baskets full.

(From Matthew 14.15, 17–20. You can also find this story in Mark 6.30–44, Luke 9.10–17 and John 6.1–14)

Pray for all those without food today, for charities, for farmers and for scientists who are working to feed the world. Think about what it must have been like to be in that crowd, and what you would have thought about Jesus at that moment.

6 Party food (a chocolate mini roll, posh biscuit, paper cup of lemonade, etc.)

Then Levi gave a great banquet for Jesus in his house . . . The Pharisees and their scribes were complaining to his disciples, saying, 'Why do you eat and drink with tax collectors and sinners?' Jesus answered, 'Those who are well have no need of a doctor, but those who are sick; I have come to call not the righteous but sinners to repentance.' Then they said to him, 'John's disciples, like the disciples of the Pharisees, frequently fast and pray, but your disciples eat and drink.' Jesus said to them, 'You cannot make wedding guests fast while the bridegroom is with them, can you?'

(Luke 5.29–34)

Imagine being at a party with Jesus. Pray that churches will welcome everyone, not just those who seem holy enough already.

7 Vinegar

When Jesus was crucified, he was given sour wine – vinegar – to drink as he was dying:

The soldiers also mocked him, coming up and offering him sour wine, and saying, 'If you are the King of the Jews, save yourself!'

(Luke 23.36–37)

Imagine seeing this happen. Pray for those who tease or persecute Christians. Pray for strength and courage for those who are suffering in any way, and for those who are dying.

8 Nine grapes/berries/ pineapple chunks

The fruit of the Spirit is love, joy, peace, patience, kindness, generosity, faithfulness, gentleness, and self-control.

(Galatians 5.22)

Pray for one of these gifts of the Spirit as you eat each piece of fruit.

Feedback

WHEN I TRIED THIS EXPERIMENT, I FOUND . . .

DOING THIS KIND OF PRAYER MADE ME FEEL . . .

THE THING I LIKED BEST ABOUT IT WAS . . .

THINGS I WOULD TRY CHANGING NEXT TIME:

MARKS OUT OF 10:

Noah's review: 3.5/10

I enjoyed eating the foods, but I didn't really feel this worked very well for me. I went round and ate the foods, and prayed for the things that were suggested, but I didn't seem to feel anything. I think the food was actually too much of a distraction: I ended up concentrating on the food rather than on the Bible verse.

The grape one was the best, because you did it again and again with each grape: as you put each one in your mouth they were small enough for me to stay focused, and the repetition of doing it nine times helped. And because I enjoy eating grapes, and they are always being represented in paintings as something luxurious, they went well with the positive ideas of love, joy and so on. That was the only one that I thought worked though.

Other experimenters' notes

8/10
- It was quite fun, I like eating stuff! Eating the honey definitely worked, it felt that those words were actually true. And I got a good vision of the party with Jesus while I was eating the party food.
- I've never tasted vinegar before! It tastes every bit as bad as you'd expect. The nine grapes was quite interesting, though I felt a bit worried that I don't have any of the gifts of the Spirit, but then I felt guilty for feeling worried...

(Members of St Mary Magdalene Church, Belmont)

7/10 - This was interesting. I tried each food and then looked up the Bible verse. I found the sweet things reminded me of the sweet things in life. I used lemon juice instead of vinegar, and that was sour and bitter and made me think of all the things that aren't so good. Doing this made me feel I could really relate to each Bible passage, and really understand it. (Reuben, 13)

8/10 – I thought this was a good idea. I think this is my favourite concept of all of these. My favourite section was the grapes, because I had a specific thing to pray about at the same time as eating the food, whereas with the others I ate the food first and then prayed. I think I focused more on the praying than on the Bible passage, but the ones where there was a short Bible passage actually written out helped me focus on that more. I felt some of the links between the passages and the food were a bit odd – the vinegar one didn't really work for me, or the party food one. I liked the fruit in the Garden of Eden one, although I'm not sure why. (Jasmine, 14)

8/10

- WE DID JUST THE LAST PART OF THIS, FOCUSING ON THE 'FRUITS OF THE SPIRIT' WITH DIFFERENT FRUITS.
- I ENJOYED IT BECAUSE YOU SPENT TIME FOCUSING ON ONE THING, THAT MADE IT COOL.
- YUMMY.
- I THINK IT IS AN UNUSUAL WAY TO PRAY.

(MEMBERS OF 'ENCOUNTER', ALL SAINTS CHURCH, HIGH WYCOMBE)

Prayer walking

Praying for a place

Prayer walking is a way of praying for a particular place or locality, when we might not know exactly what the people who live there need, or even who they are. It can be a way of praying for the streets near your home, or it can be used by a church group to pray for a place that they feel is in special need of prayer.

In prayer walking, two ancient traditions of prayer are combined: intercession and pilgrimage. The first thing you might think of when you think about prayer is praying for God to help other people. This is called 'intercession', asking God to act on behalf of people or situations which we believe need God's help.

But we can often feel overwhelmed and confused by how much there is to pray for. And sometimes we don't know what is needed, so it is hard to know how to put it into words. This can be especially tricky when we want to pray for a particular place, perhaps the area around where we live, or around our church, or somewhere that has had a lot of problems recently. We won't always know who all the people are that we are praying for, and the problems a place has may be very complicated.

Pilgrimage and prayer walking

Then there is the ancient tradition of pilgrimage, going on a journey to a holy place as an act of self-dedication. Pilgrimages were usually undertaken on foot, so they meant that you were committing a significant amount of time and effort. The point wasn't to pray a lot on the way, the very act of undertaking the pilgrimage was the act of prayer. As in pilgrimage, the very fact of walking means that we are 'walking the walk not just talking the talk'. We aren't just saying prayers, we are expressing our care for the place we are praying for physically, by walking around it. We are putting ourselves to some effort, not just sitting comfortably at home. And the action of walking takes up some of our conscious mind, so that prayer can flow more freely without us worrying too much about our exact words.

The main difference between this kind of walking and pilgrimage is that for prayer walking there doesn't need to be a particular destination in mind. Instead of walking to get somewhere, in this kind of prayer the walk itself, up and down the local streets, through the park or past the shops, is the point. You could, of course, choose to walk to a particular place, maybe a park, viewpoint or church, but the point of this exercise is not getting there, but praying for the places you pass through and think about on the way.

The experiment

YOU CAN DO THIS WALK EITHER ALONE OR IN A SMALL GROUP, MAYBE WITH A FRIEND FROM CHURCH. IN CHOOSING WHERE TO GO, THINK ABOUT YOUR SAFETY AND THE PRACTICALITIES OF TRAFFIC AND FOOTPATHS. I SUGGEST YOU BEGIN BY WALKING AROUND YOUR LOCAL AREA – THE STREETS AROUND YOUR HOUSE, SCHOOL OR CHURCH – BUT IF THIS IS NOT PRACTICAL OR SAFE THEN PLAN TO GO SOMEWHERE ELSE. CHOOSE AN AREA THAT YOU ARE FAMILIAR WITH – MAYBE WHERE A GRANDPARENT OR A FRIEND LIVES, OR SOMEWHERE YOU GO TO FOR SHOPPING OR ANOTHER ACTIVITY. BEFORE SETTING OFF, PLAN YOUR ROUTE AND TELL SOMEONE WHERE YOU ARE GOING AND WHEN TO EXPECT YOU BACK (A BASIC SAFETY PRECAUTION).

As you walk, pray – not out loud, just in your head – for the places you are passing. You might ask God to bless the people who live in the houses you pass. If you go past a school, or shops, or offices, you could pray for the people who work there, and for all that they do. A particular business might make you think of things to pray for: a supermarket might spark off a thought about fair trade, or struggling farmers, or those who can't afford food easily. A newsagent might make you think about people in the news, or about the people reading their papers at home and what they are worrying about. A florist might remind you to pray for people who will be buying flowers this week to celebrate, or to mourn.

If you pass churches or other places of worship, pray for the people who meet there. Depending on your local situation you might also want to pray about particular community tensions, or for church projects.

Just let thoughts arise in your mind, and when you notice that you are thinking about something, pray for it.

There will probably be people passing you, on foot or bicycle, in cars and buses. You might pray for God's Holy Spirit to fill the lady who passes you walking her dog, or for the man just leaving the shop across the road to be aware of God's presence with him. If an ambulance goes past, pray for the paramedics and whoever they are going to help. A delivery van might make you think of praying for anyone whose birthday it is today, or for those who are lonely and never get letters or parcels.

As you return home, ask God to bless the whole locality, and to show you how you can be a blessing to it. You might like to end by praying for your own home as you enter it.

173

Feedback

WHEN I TRIED THIS EXPERIMENT, I FOUND . . .

DOING A PRAYER WALK MADE ME FEEL . . .

THE THING I LIKED BEST ABOUT IT WAS . . .

THINGS I WOULD TRY CHANGING NEXT TIME:

MARKS OUT OF 10:

174

Noah's review: 7.5/10

For my first prayer walk, I decided to go somewhere different. Instead of walking where I live I went with a friend around the area where he lives. As I walked around I discovered places I hadn't been to before. It was a very run-down area and I spent most of my walk praying for the area and the people who lived there. I didn't just pray for the town and the people in the houses but also for people who are maybe stressed and troubled. And for a bit of my walk I prayed for the people waiting at the bus stop in the pouring rain.

It was kind of weird doing it with a friend: in a way it felt slightly awkward because I wanted to talk with him but he was praying, and he probably wanted to talk to me but knew I was praying. But it was nice too, because I knew someone else was praying for people and he was right there with me.

Then a few weeks later I tried this again in the area where I live, on my own. I got lost in a housing estate, which I guess was good, because there were places I hadn't seen before and I realized there was a lot of the area I didn't know about. There were some old people sitting reading so I prayed for them as I went past, that they would have a happy life, and some children playing outside with a ball, so I prayed for them as well. There were also some builders who looked like they were having a rough time doing some building work, so I prayed that they were safe in their job and that God would look over them. At points where there weren't individual people I prayed for the street or the houses I was passing – just saying 'I pray for this street'.

It was quite nice: it felt much less selfish than praying sometimes does. I often pray for myself and for other people in countries that are in conflict or in times of need, but it was much nicer praying for people closer to home who probably still needed praying for. I would recommend doing it by yourself or with one other person, but probably not with a large group – thinking about doing it with my church youth group I think that would be weird, as we'd be walking round in a big group but not speaking to each other, which wouldn't feel very sociable.

Other experimenters' notes

8/10 – The prayer walk not only allowed me to learn more about myself, but also about the place where I live. It's a way to pray in a no-stress environment, and good for blessing on the go. Personally, I found it different and enjoyable. I found walking and praying wasn't as restrictive as praying in a church. In a building you don't feel with God as much, I feel like I'm in a place built by people, not any kind of powerful force. Going outside into the world he created feels like you are actually with God in the world he made. (Harry, 13)

10/10 – I WALKED A SHORT WAY TO MY GRAN'S HOUSE ON THE SAME STREET. IT MADE ME FEEL LUCKY TO LIVE IN A NICE HOUSE. I THOUGHT ABOUT THE PEOPLE LIVING IN THE HOUSES I PASSED AND PRAYED FOR THE LIVES THEY ARE LIVING AND THE PEOPLE I KNOW. I THOUGHT ABOUT THE CHILDREN SUFFERING IN WARS IN THE NEWS AT THE MOMENT, AND HOW I FEEL SAFE IN MY COMMUNITY. I LIKED PRAYING FOR THE PEOPLE I KNOW. IT MADE ME FEEL MORE AWARE OF PEOPLE IN OTHER COMMUNITIES. (EMMA, 11)

9/10 – I really liked this. It was really good, and made me feel closer to nature.

I took the dog with me to a big field near my house, and walked round that. I didn't really pray on the way there, just as I was walking round the field – it just felt natural to do that, I felt more free in the field rather than in the streets. I kind of prayed about nature and things. There were lots of trees, and green and space, and it made me feel grateful for it all and closer to it. Having the dog with me was really nice too, I threw a ball for her and prayed for her a bit. That made me feel more connected to her too.

I think I will try this again in different places, like in the woods. I feel more comfortable with the idea of praying while I'm walking in natural surroundings: I can't really imagine doing this in the streets round where I live. But now I come to think of it, it might be quite fun to do it in places like central London. (Jasmine, 14)

The authors

Miranda and Noah Threlfall-Holmes are a mum and son based in
Durham, in north-east England.

Noah is 13 years old, and attends Durham Johnston Comprehensive
School in Durham. A laid-back character, he proudly describes
himself as a bit of a nerd. He enjoys video games, especially playing
online with friends; reading books by authors such as Charlie Higson
and Philip Reeve, and Manga graphic novels; and playing Pokemon.
A Scout patrol leader, he is particularly skilled at map reading and
navigating. His favourite subjects at school are Geography and
Mandarin. For the past four years, he has been a regular at the CPAS
'Stagefright' venture week, exploring faith through drama, and he
also enjoys attending Greenbelt and the 'Totally Awesome Youth
Club' of St Mary Magdalene Church, Belmont.

Miranda is 41 years old, and is Vicar of St Mary Magdalene, Belmont,
and St Laurence, Pittington. She is not a laid-back character. She
first worked in brand management and was then a historian before
ordination, and holds first-class degrees in history from Cambridge
and theology from Durham, and a PhD in medieval monastic history.
Her publications include *The Essential History of Christianity* (SPCK,
2012), *Being a Chaplain* (SPCK, 2011), *Monks and Markets: Durham
Cathedral Priory, 1460–1520* (OUP, 2005), poems, and articles in
the church and popular press. She trained for ministry at Cranmer
Hall, Durham, served her title at St Gabriel, Heaton in Newcastle

diocese, and was Chaplain of University College, Durham, and Interim Principal of Ustinov College, Durham, before taking up her current post in 2012. She has been a member of the Church of England's General Synod and Vice-Chair of Women and the Church (WATCH). She enjoys felting, reading murder mysteries and Regency romances (and trying to write a murder mystery), and gardening. She has been married to Phil, a chemical engineer, for 18 years, and they have three children, of whom Noah is the eldest.

Acknowledgements

This book started life as a blog, in which Miranda wrote an idea for prayer each week, and then Noah tried it out and blogged about how he had found it. As the blog got more popular, the ideas began to be used by individuals and church youth groups around the country, and many of them have generously contributed feedback to this book.

We would particularly like to thank the following for experimenting, for sharing their feedback with us and with you, and for being so open, honest and thoughtful in describing how it was for them:

Jasmine Bennett, Reuben Cook, Rachel Moberly, Daniel Rix, Luke Nichols, Emily Robson, Callum Cullingworth, Hazel Cullingworth, Edward Bradshaw, Catherine Bradshaw, Daisy Bradshaw, Jonny Halliday, Dan Halliday, Harry Little, Hannah Lewis, Emma Arnold, Phoebe Wakefield, Emily Wilson, Beatrice Dickinson; Ruth Harley and the members of 'Encounter', All Saints Church, High Wycombe; Kat and Tim Marjoriebanks and the members of 'Deeper', St John's Church, Neville's Cross, Durham; Grace Thomas and the members of '3Generate'; Blackburn Cathedral Confirmation Group; Colum and Lizzie Goodchild and the members of the 'Totally Awesome Youth Club' of St Mary Magdalene, Belmont, Durham.

Thanks also to Mina Munns, creator of the Flame Creative Kids website, for permission to include one of her colouring sheets

ACKNOWLEDGEMENTS

here; to Lindsay Southern for the Nerf gun confession idea; to Rachel Moberly for the prayer den idea; to Tracey Messenger at SPCK for her advice and support; and to the rest of our family, Phil, Tobias and Zoe Threlfall-Holmes, for their patience, help, comments and support over the past year as we have written this book.